# Untethered in Paradise

For Christina
the Sunday mood
of life

L. Welch
March 2002

**ACKNOWLEDGMENTS**

Several of the prose texts have appeared or are to appear in altered versions in: *Estuaires, Galerie, The Nashwaak Review, The New Brunswick Reader.*

Some of the poems were first published in different versions or in their present form in *Fidelities, The Rock's Stillness* and *Unlearning Ice.*

A salute of gratitude to all the unconditionally generous friends in Europe and North America.

Special thanks to Glenn Clever, Marie-Anne Hansen, Marnie Parsons, Frank Tierney, Tina Wüstemann for their unfailing support and guidance.

Photograph of author by Cyril Welch.

Front cover image by Alex Colville, *Surveyor* (2001, acrylic, 36 x 63.2 cm).

Back cover image by Gust Graas, *"fuelled by our blue cold"* (2000, oil on paper, 15 x 21 cm).

*For Cyril*

*who tends the clearing*

## BOOKS BY LILIANE WELCH

### Poetry

*Winter Songs* (1977) chapbook
*Syntax of Ferment* (1979)
*Assailing Beats* (1979)
*October Winds* (1980)
*Brush and Trunks* (1981)
*From the Songs of the Artisans* (1983)
*Unrest Bound* (1985) chapbook
*Manstorna: Life on the Mountain* (1985)
*Word-House of a Grandchild* (1987)
*A Taste for Words* (1988) chapbook
*Fire to the Looms Below* (1990)
*Life in Another Language* (1992)
*Von Menschen und Orten* (1992)
*Dream Museum* (1995)
*Fidelities* (1997)
*Mosaics: Music Scapes Words* (1998)
*The Rock's Stillness* (1999)
*Unlearning Ice* (2001)

### Literary Criticism

*Emergence: Baudelaire, Mallarmé, Rimbaud* (1973) with C.
    Welch
*Address: Rimbaud, Mallarmé, Butor* (1979) with C. Welch


### Prose

*Seismographs: Selected Essays and Reviews* (1988)
*Frescoes: Travel Pieces* (1998)

# Untethered

## *in* Paradise

Liliane Welch

Borealis Press
Ottawa, Canada
2002

## Canadä

The Publishers acknowledge the financial assistance of the
Government of Canada through the Book Publishing
Program (BPIDP) for our publishing activities.

**National Library of Canada Cataloguing in Publication
Data**

Welch, Liliane, 1937-
    Untethered in paradise

ISBN 0-88887-204-6

1. Title.

PS8595.E54U68  2002      C811'.54          C2002-900622-8
PR9199.3.W416U68 2002

Cover: design by Bull's Eye Design, Ottawa, Canada,
using Author's photo.
Other acknowledgements on p. ii, are an extension of this
copyright page.

*Printed and bound in Canada on acid free paper*

CONTENTS

# Foreword

All our lives the people we love most, our family, our friends, like to share with us our pleasures, to point out beauty, to offer information, to be at once a friend and a teacher. Even toddlers are taught through the sharing of pleasure. The names of things, yes, but, as well our responses, both sensuous and cultural. We say to a child: "That flower is a rose. Isn't it pretty! Roses are red; violets are blue; angels in heaven know I love you!" Other poems later will further freight the rose. In a sense, we learn to "see" through the eyes, the memories, the responses of others.

The arts, by offering us a vision not our own, enlarge our own vision, and, thus, enlarge our lives. Yet, however rich an experience it may be to confront great works of art alone and unpreparedly, we are generally very happy to share this experience with others, and, even more, delighted to have an informed and responsive guide to help us "see" through their eyes, their memories, their responses.

In *Untethered in Paradise* Liliane Welch joins the company of such valued guides who, sharing with us their experiences of beauty, teach us to see more fully. The paradise of Welch's title is the paradise of art, of earthly life as revealed in its mysterious sanctity through great paintings and sculptures.

*Untethered in Paradise* invites us to accompany Welch as she recollects and describes her encounters and responses to the works of favored artists: Rodin, Cézanne, Chardin, Monet, Giovanni and Alberto Giacometti, Lotto, Caravaggio, Vermeer, Colville, Gust Graas. Placing herself as viewer in

ix

our contemporary world — as traveller, reader, lover of mountains and flowers — she offers for each a contextual encounter in prose. She brings to these encounters a wonderful supply of brilliant perceptive remarks made by writers, philosophers, and artists that illuminate for her and for us, the works encountered. Following each encounter, she distills her responses in poems, a tribute by one art to another.

Welch's work is at once a tribute and an excursion. We travel with her, we read with her, we look with her. In her various responses Welch refers to many of the themes that recur when we contemplate the lives and works of artists: the problem of solitude and unpopularity, the sense of isolation, the necessity of endurance. She reminds us of the affirmative and renewing qualities of great art: how great art can communicate a human and spiritual warmth — how, in its weighty and mysterious silences, it speaks to us. As Welch says of Colville's paintings: "We are inspired to cross the hidden barrier of everyday experience, entering into things radiating discreetly and luminously in an endless conversation . . . ."

The conversations in *Untethered in Paradise* are multi-sided. Rilke, Wilde, Baudelaire, Rimbaud, Nietzsche, Proust . . . famous voices join us as, led by Welch, we consider these glorious paintings and statues, appreciating both art and the source of art, the beauty of nature. It is impossible to read this book without wanting to re-read the writers quoted, to review the works seen. It is impossible to read this companionable book without feeling a surge of friendship for so congenial and responsive a guide.

M. Travis Lane
Fredericton, N.B., 2002

# I

# LUXEMBOURG:

# THE CLANDESTINE RODIN

## A MOSAIC OF BLACK STONES

When I was an adolescent in Luxembourg in the early 1950s, an art professor showed us reproductions of Rodin's statues. He was the one great sculptor she knew and loved, and her enthusiasm infected me. I coveted those sculptures all the more because in my parents' house images of the nude human body were considered lascivious, sinful. Rodin became a constant companion. What his statues said changed me: looking at them I knew that I didn't want to end up having simply visited the world.

Rodin, my clandestine hero. From him I learned that art is a place to enter. His naked children satisfied my youthful hunger to defy the Roman Church's preaching. The power and affirmation of his sculptures kept me buoyant, revelling in their passion and faith, despite the moralistic interdicts of priests and nuns. On solitary walks through the woods of my hometown, my mind would turn to him, and be delivered from the closed-mindedness and bigotry that permeated my society.

How struck I was when in my early thirties I saw the splendid portrait of Rodin by Edward Steichen, a photographer born in Luxembourg but raised in America; some fifty years prior to my own infatuation he became Rodin's promoter in America. The whole of Rodin is condensed in that simple silhouette cast darkly against the massive white marble of his Victor Hugo. Perhaps I was magnetized by the electricity of what Oscar Wilde called Rodin's "dreams in marble." Or, like Rilke, intrigued by an artist whose "destiny was to work as Nature works, not as men."

Already as a girl I sensed in the reproductions an extraordinary push, some compulsive excitement; now as a young woman I was drawn to him as a man apart, a loner, a tireless worker. Ill at ease in the company of others, even with friends he seemed disconnected from his surroundings — the room became "filled with the weight of his silence," Helen von Hindenburg remembered. At night, in Meudon, when he meditated before the landscape, no small talk was allowed; then his only mistresses were nature and aloneness. Incessant labours filled his days. He lived what his father had taught him as a young boy: "Think about words such as: energy — will — determination. Then you will be victorious." Once he admitted: "... as soon as I stop working I am bored; not to produce would be odious for me. Rest is monotonous and has the sadness of all things that come to an end." A dogged, isolated life, but the achievements that grew out of it are titanic.

Yet no artist was more contested and insulted than Rodin. Battles raged around his works for forty years: rejections, vitriolic attacks, public derision without cease. Outbursts against his person and art dominated the press and were even carried into the French Senate, where champions of academic art thundered against what they took to be "mental aberrations," but which many since consider the renewal of sculpture. The reactionary official state guardians of French culture would not tolerate his reinterpretation and revitalization of the tradition. Amazingly, throughout the almost inconceivable indignities he suffered, his certitude never flagged, his faith never lessened. He must have been dismayed but he did not change his course.

Perhaps this divine seriousness in adversity kept him an abiding presence in my own life; I gravitated on numerous occasions to the Rodin Museums in Paris and Philadelphia, and the gallery of his statues at the New York Metropolitan Museum, often pondering his phrase: "Life is a mosaic of black stones." Over the years, his works have evolved for me, from an aphrodisiac to a beacon, to something more complex than both. Looking back, I see that over fifty years I've never lost sight of *The Kiss*, *The Thinker* and *Balzac*. Those statues were and are Rodin for me.

As an adolescent I exalted at the lustre of *The Kiss* in mere reproduction; it invited me into a forbidden theatre of sensual caresses and frenzied desire. Later, in museums, the same sculpture touched a deeper chord: that kiss so hot, the fire of passion so bright, the rapture of those two bodies transfigured into the ecstasy of truly intimate partnership.

*The Thinker* summoned me differently. I saw in the athletic figure first a celebration of the muscular bodies of the miners and steel workers who populated the streets of my home town. Later, married to a philosopher, I understood how, in this giant who sits silently and thinks with every muscle in his body, Rodin captured the bone-deep kinship between thought and action, their common root in solitude. The *Thinker* glorifies the human task of meditating on the gift of life.

With his *Balzac*, Rodin altered irrevocably contemporary art. In my youth, without knowing exactly why, I was strongly attracted to the broad, striding body lost in a cloak, head thrown back, a veritable menhir. Later in America, I marvelled at how Rodin was engrossed for years in Balzac, how he put vast energies into visiting the writer's home in Touraine, reading his letters, living his novels, collecting words from his contemporaries, filling himself with that man's very spirit before he created the statue enwrapped in silence and elemental power. Rodin confided to Paul Gsell that with this figure he wanted to create a genius capable of reconstructing "the entire structure of his society and to expose life in all its tumultuousness for his contemporaries and for all generations to come." *Balzac*, the artist challenging life with his own vitality, has mentored me and stood beside me through my own commitment to writing.

Yet precisely this grandiose figure unleashed the most vicious campaign of vilification against Rodin. For one critic it was a mere "polar bear standing on his hind legs." For others it provided yet another occasion to vent hatreds pent up against an artist who invented a new language of art. Today it is hard to comprehend how *Balzac*, Rodin's best and last great monument, the bedrock of his creative life, could occasion such rage. Did this statue once and for all put the lie to those who wanted to reduce art to the depiction of mythological and historical subjects? Did this *Balzac*, the incarnation of man as creator, threaten the existence of the French art establishment? Were the attacks a refrain sung by those who had called *The Thinker* an "angry orangutan . . . an enormous brute . . . chewing his cud"? Only a few years after the Balzac affair, in 1916, those same enemies of the artist used with equal exasperation every device of infamy to prevent the creation of the Rodin Museum in Paris.

Long before I wrote and loved, I rushed excitedly toward Rodin's statues, and through them into imaginations of the body's pleasures. They returned me to an innocent delight, hope and faith. They told me that a better life was open somewhere, sometime. They summoned me to look, think and feel the height of bodied joy. This was Rodin's first gift to me. For didn't I want to be, at times, exactly like his statues? The lover who adores another? The thinker who sits in the clearing of mystery? The creator whose energy miraculously changes life?

Sometimes now, Rodin's work extends before me as a mountainous landscape where he urgently invites me to rise out of dailiness into an awakening experience. If *The Kiss* is rapture, if *The Thinker* is luminosity, if *Balzac* is creation, the entire body of Rodin's work is thunderous in its joyful affirmation, in its call to take on another sight, to step from ordinary life into a new light. To have represented this possibility of paradise is the *tour de force*, the miracle that Rodin achieved. His sculptures look at me with the bravado of life's force itself.

**The marble couple gleams**

You have known them
forever, open to promise
where his hand shapes her thigh.
Your words — gathered — search
for home.  The kiss
transfigures you, you stand
beside your partner.

The Rodin Museum in Paris:
all those seductive bodies, so few
eyes to rehearse the nude light.

Love without end or deception.

**When we glimpse them, delight**

our palms tingle because their hands don't touch;
we live the man and woman shouldering out
of marble, leaving darkness.
As children, we did push clay,
that art of finger-love. Now
the couple vibrates in us, he rising
to bury his face in her breast, she leaning
back, in reverie, to accept
his kiss. Observe,
says a guide in the Paris museum,
facing visitors, Rodin
was moulding torso-language.
We stand behind them in the busy hall,
divining an imperious titan shape,
fire in the hush of stone —
until it occupies us.
Adoration takes over,
in that kneeling embrace, glowing, growing
like our own awakening, warding
off loneliness.
                And love,
when consummated, is it two bodies held
by ancient fulfillment,
or a mountain's radiance, stirring
in an eternal idol's hands?

# II

# FRANCE:

# KNIGHTS OF THE CANVAS

## THE FIRE WITHIN THE STONE

"Never since Moses has anyone seen a mountain so greatly." Rilke's phrase dogs me. We are driving through the ancient countryside of Provence, its magnificence cultivated as well as ignored for ages. A pagan magic fills the side roads, classical Mediterranean culture struggling on in sea-air and earth. We have come to stay a few days at Aix, Cézanne's home ground, to capture a mountain's passage to artwork, a man's passage to priest. But also to have our eyes leap into a new light.

Capitalizing on the great master, today Aix calls itself "the city of Cézanne." It is a town of outdoor life, medieval fortifications, palace gates through which the perfume of aristocracy wafts, stone relics from the heady past. Even so, lawless young motorcyclists terrorize the dusty streets, and according to our hotel clerk, cars with foreign license plates are best stored in the underground parking—behind two doors which open only upon insertion of a secret code. The clerk's warning explains why at the toll stations on the "Sun Highway" we saw armed policemen surveying the traffic, and why vehicles with four gendarmes patrolled the roadside resting places.

What remains of Cézanne in Aix today? When in the 1980s land developers threatened to tear down the studio Cézanne had constructed at Les Lauves in 1901, the American writer James Lord raised funds to restore it and open it for

public visitation.  Since then the Granet museum also has on
permanent loan from the French government eight paintings —
if they are not travelling with other exhibitions; recently it
acquired one drawing and an aquarelle.  Are the town fathers
atoning for the curator who, while Cézanne was still painting,
vowed that during his own lifetime no canvas of that
"lamentable failure" would profane the walls of his fiefdom?
Once Cézanne died and achieved belated celebrity, the public
dismay and abuse ebbed away.  The Tourist Bureau of Aix
has reinstated the scorned artist with a three kilometre long
pedestrian circuit — on which 2,500 bronze studs in the
pavement, each bearing a "C," lead tourists to the places
Cézanne frequented.  Outside the city a further itinerary
guides one to the artist's favourite painting spots.  From there
one can snap photos of Mont Sainte-Victoire and compare
them later to the postcard reproductions for sale at every
newsstand in town.

For thirty years, Cézanne's life consisted of nothing but
work.  He was at his easel from 6:00 a.m. till sundown, with
only short breaks for lunch and Sunday mass.  Progressing
slowly, he needed months for each painting and hundreds of
sittings from his models.  In the end, the eternal presence of
Mont Sainte-Victoire and of the old gardener Vallier were a
blessing; both were just there, would not get up and leave.

The story of Cézanne's life at Aix, and earlier in Paris,
is one of constant misunderstandings.  He told his coachman:
"The world does not understand me.  And I do not understand
the world.  That is why I have withdrawn from it."  Mauled
by journalists and peers, threatened by letters from the
burghers of Aix, pelted with stones by their children, sick and
old, he wrote: "To work without worrying about anyone, and

becoming strong, that's the aim of the artist." Simultaneously he wondered: "Is art indeed a priesthood that demands the pure in heart, completely dedicated to it?"

I know him from two photos. One in 1904, an old man sitting with folded hands before the huge canvas "The Bathers," his black pants splattered with paint, his gaze austere, intent. The second from 1906, shortly before his death. He stands outside at his easel in black suit and bowler hat, grim, doggedly aflame for his mountain. In both images a colossal solitude. This obstinate old recluse knew that he was made for isolation, for venerating the "configurations" of his countryside. His love for the Midi burned intensely under its shimmering heat, amidst cicada song, while Aix dozed below.

These two photographs remind me of another. Martin Heidegger in 1968: his back turned to us, a beret on his head, he looks at Mont Sainte-Victoire. The greatest thinker of our time, on pilgrimage to Aix. Heidegger felt an affinity with the painter, and in a poem commemorated the silence in Cézanne's painting of the humble gardener Vallier, "who tended inconspicuous things near the Lauves road."

Walking into the sun-filled day toward Mont Sainte-Victoire, one sees toward the south a high plateau wrapped in a Virgilian peace. This was once a hub of Greek learning, Caesar's romanized Gaul. The swaying pines along the way speak the language of Cézanne's canvases. The old painter's worship still adheres to them. Bright red poppy fields stare at the sky. To the north, the mountain is bounded by naked stony scrub, a wildness and solitude like that of the artist-priest Cézanne.

As a youth, with his companions Zola and Baile, Cézanne avoided the common pleasures of loitering in cafés and streets, roamed instead through this natural terrain, drunk on the baked red earth, aromatic herbs, resinous trees, the brooks, vineyards and olive trees shepherded by the blue-white peak of Mont Sainte-Victoire. In the wilds of that lost paradise, Cézanne's eyes became schooled for the extraordinary seeing preserved in his paintings. Here he practised the boundless loyalty of the artist that Rilke repeatedly likened to an old dog:

> ...the dog of his work that is calling him again and that beats him and lets him starve. And yet he's attached with his whole being to this incomprehensible master who only lets him return to the Lord on Sundays, as if to his original owner, just for a while.

Closer to Mont Sainte-Victoire, 1 remember Renoir calling Cézanne's wildness that of a bristling "porcupine." He prowled this countryside, swollen on pine cones, ballooned on lavender and sage, dragging his yearning over the dry mud, alchemizing it near the mountain, scared that "others would put their claws into him." He chuckled to himself when the colours of his canvas vibrated with the earth's sweetness, was terrorized when humans crowded in to distract or touch him, bored by social talk, impressed by sweat gleaming on the haunted face of Vallier. He enthroned that faithful gardener on a simple wooden chair under the linden tree, and the mountain kept watch over both.

We too become dogs and porcupines as we spring up a little knoll, gnawing out these images, starved, seeking revelation among stubby thistles. We flee into the mineral whiteness of Cézanne's summit, where shadows from clouds pull curtains over the steep wall, and bumblebees labour in the cracks.

Although not the highest mountain of Provence, Mont Sainte-Victoire is the most abrupt. A chain of summits roughly 1,000 metres high, it stretches over the hilly land. Only from Aix does it look like a peak, its gleaming dolomite limestone lending it a white glistening appearance. No road leads onto it, no inn stands near it. On its windy crest visited by swifts, sits an abandoned hermit's chapel from the 17th century. The mountain's south wall is a climber's paradise.

Cézanne painted Mont Sainte-Victoire more than sixty times. His brush revisited each of its shapes, its jagged masses, bulwarks, the heaviness of its rocks, until the mountain lent meaning to his life, became his promised land. He was restored to equilibrium when he submitted to it, had "folded its erring hands." His colours caressed one layer of the rock after another, and ecstasy grabbed him. He fervently believed that natural things, like fruits and stones, talked with each other, that they approached human beings to tell them about the fields where they grew, about the rains that nourished them, the dawns they spied upon.

At noon, we are the lone hikers atop the crest. We salute the Mediterranean to the south, Mont Ventoux, Petrarch's mountain to the north. At 2:00, we leave Mont Sainte-Victoire for the sweltering valley. After his youth Cézanne never again climbed the mountain. He remained at a painterly distance, often at Le Tholonet, a small village east of Aix. There we find a small café, sit on the terrace under plane trees, and watch an old Frenchman speak with his dog. By the time we are ready for the last leg of our journey, it is after 4:00. The heat has abated, the light no longer vibrates savagely. This is the hour Cézanne prized above all. Then he went far out into the field to paint. Soon the shadows grow longer, the air turns limpid and crystalline. The mountain we have left behind takes on a peculiar sharpness; the road glows with the withdrawing sun.

That hour is more memorable than the short time we linger next day in Cézanne's studio at Les Lauves. How many visitors have poured through this now-public space? The artist's remaining still-life utensils are vestiges of something withheld, momentarily creating the illusion that we are close to him. But later, dropping out of Cézanne's life, under the high arched plane trees of the Cours Mirabeau with its fountains and crowds, we realize that his art was missing at the studio. It somehow refused to be held in those rooms. Cézanne, the mountain's messenger, had fled.

A month after we leave Aix, Cézanne's holy mountain is in attendance again on the walls of museums in Basel and Zurich. Time stands still. Bluffs, ravines, dark energy shimmers from the canvases with the freshness of the first day of creation. Afloat in southern light, paradise regained. The solitary majesty of the peak rises toward heaven together with Cézanne's devotion to its manifold presence. We "drink these paintings," as their maker recommended. Then, at last, we fathom with what conviction the old hermit let himself be possessed by the fire which burned inside the stones. He became the landscape's consciousness. We head with him from that world of vertical colours into his last letter to his son: "I continue to work with difficulty, but in spite of that something is achieved."

**Victory**

*Paul Cézanne (1839 - 1906)*

On such a morning of glitter he died,
    a pure-toned October day.
Here the embrace of earth and sky,
    of fire, daringly

reaching toward his crystalline peak,
    rhapsodic, through shimmering blues,
greens, violets and purples, to divine
    the rock's stillness

that messenger who arrests to shift
    the semaphores of passion.
An ancient breath of silence descends
    over hands still painting;

Mont Sainte-Victoire dances with the wind.
    O faithful monk of Aix,
mark for us with your palette
    the high rooms of the dark.

## Nudes in a Landscape
*Photograph, 1904*

Although the eight women bathers
unveil their last shyness in the painting's wood,
their soft breasts
discreet pillows, intimate and casual;

although the cloud
hovers beyond like a voyeur
endlessly patient; although the picnic
baskets might invite him
to share their ancient rites,

Cézanne, all in black, seated
before the blue-green canvas folds
his hands and gazes away,
as if the ceremony of these figures
were holding the whole world's eyes.

## Small Steps

Cézanne's old gardener
is the artist in repose. Will he
cultivate in us a different seeing?

Athlete of moist soil: his hands,
tools, face are
a sweet-water well.

Now the stool is a throne of meditation,
his crossed legs, roots beyond time,
indentured to ground.

That straw hat
a halo gathering heaven,
the linden tree, an umbrella,

anchor to the sun.
And the espadrilles,
the feet's canvas gloves caressing

the lover's naked back.
They live only small steps:
to the flower bed, the water can.

Look. His
white beard makes him
a Moses:

colour's prophet,
the Promised Land a canvas,
the transport of work.

## Quick Flights

My favorite Cézanne portrait:  Hortense,
his wife erect in a yellow armchair.
Hands twisted, unfinished on her red lap,
eyes drunk on void, and from behind a black
band saying it will strap her pout into
the longing of any viewer's stare.
Quick flights from life's terrors, blocked
cries, ravenous wiles capsizing like sails.
And it's in Zurich's Kunsthaus, in spacious rooms,
the slow lapping and sway of visitor streams,
that I recall her saying, "Cézanne didn't
know what he was doing." And imagine
her sitting for hours before him, still
as an apple, gambling tables locked inside.

## CÉZANNE'S HEROES

When the Museum of Fine Art in Basel recently presented an exhibition featuring as "guest of honour" Cézanne's *Still Life with Apples and Peaches,* I felt doubly attracted to the Swiss city on the Rhine: to its natural setting, the bridges and ferries, and at the outskirts the meadows ringing with bells of cows; and to its veneration of art. Not only the extraordinary masterpieces astound, but also the generosity of the donours who legated these treasures to public institutions. Moreover, there reigns a modern spirit in the Basel museums, rather than bored or cranky guards, men and women dressed to their own taste mix discretely with the viewers. Thus the handsome young banker, the student in T-shirt, or the smiling middle-aged woman turn out to wear small badges as overseers.

Cézanne, the wild peasant from Provence, would have approved. The dusty Granet museum in his hometown, Aix-en-Provence, would not please him anymore today than it did in 1900 — uniformed old men, fused to chairs, seem to wait out the day for closing time. They could be the deformed librarians in Rimbaud's poem "The Seated Ones." Perhaps they know that thieves would not remove the *pièces de résistance* under their care; the kitsch in vogue during Cézanne's lifetime now hangs to the high ceiling of the penumbral gallery.

When I look at the painted apples and peaches in Basel, I taste the sweet, sharp tang of Canadian fruits on my tongue.

I understand Cézanne's exclamation: "With an apple I want to surprise Paris." In heaps of fruit he painted the mysteries of light and growth, dawn and evening. In more than 170 still lifes, he made vases, pitchers, towels, drapes and fruits his protagonists, rendering them visible to our befogged eyes. In each one of those paintings ordinary things begin to speak. Their lapidary, silent concision radiates with a lyrical outer finish as well as with the cadence of nature. At home in Cézanne's canvases these utensils and fruits cast an unforgettable spell.

The guest of honour painting in Basel bears two names, *Still Life with Apples and Peaches* and *Nature morte au vase pique-fleurs*. They declare emblematically the bond between natural and man-made things. A large oil on canvas, 81 x 100 cm, this is the last of Cézanne's still life studies, a genre to which he lent new force. On a plain kitchen table of light wood with a baroquely cut front apron, fruits gleam, a milk jug with flower pattern nestles in drapery which flows down and is relayed by a white cloth, while in the background a *vase pique-fleurs* stands. On the table's uncovered portion on the right is a plate, piled high with glistening, freshly picked apples and peaches. The warm golden yellows, orange, ochre and brown tints invite one to stroke the smooth and furry skins. I can hear Cézanne saying: "If one circumscribes with full lines the skin of a beautiful peach, the melancholy of an old apple, one divines in their shared reflexes the same shadow of renunciation, the same love of sunshine, the same remembrance of dew, a freshness."

The eye wanders next to the *vase pique-fleurs*, a vase with holes to insert flowers, whose pink and light blue shades contrast with the dark, brownish background. Its emptiness recalls the perfume of absent flowers and points to the drapery cascade over the left half of the table. The blue-green and ochre patterns of this curtain could be a heap of rocks. The purplish flower motif of the milk pitcher could be the foliage of fruit trees rising now out of the stones. Meanwhile, on the table just below the heavy brocade drapery a white cloth flows like an impetuous mountain stream into the depth of the foreground.

*Still Life with Apples and Peaches* organizes the visible also into a dramatic architecture. A geometry of trapezes and pyramids sends the eye to every corner of the art work, onto all those fruits and utensils, which we use blindly every day. I'm persuaded  that the secret heart of things resides in a simple, small yellow apple which rests on a pile of peaches, and recall Cézanne's remark:  "What I have never and will never attain in the human figure or in the portrait, perhaps I touched it in the still life."

Cézanne's still lifes lay bare the sinews of painting as well as the energies of reality. Their brush strokes bespeak an immediacy that presses like hot metal against the retina. Infected by his passion, I feel re-oriented, admitted to that promised land where ordinary perceptions dissipate. The travels I longed for all winter reverberate here, in this still life:  Europe's smell of bread, coffee, tobacco and car exhaust, its uncomfortable hotel beds, its cats sharpening their claws on barn doors, our triumph upon subduing an infuriated dog.

Yet such ephemera vanish before Cézanne's miraculous fortitude in the face of public failure. Like him I too can "see with joy," travel from the presence of the painted things to their inner light and stillness. It is as though the apples and peaches remembered the sun that ripened them, the pitcher the fire that baked its mud, the table the tree from which it was cut. The peasant within me craves growth, nature. On the canvas everything is alive, awaiting a sign. Drapes transmute into an avalanche of stones, and on the homey table there gleam ruby apples, topaz yellow peaches, a crystal stream of white cloth.

The still life makes me responsive to the freshness, the matinal dress of the things nearest us. Even though I cannot be a painter for whom "seeing is conceiving and conceiving is composing," I thank Cézanne. He has re-oriented me from imposition to response. The fleeting mystery of an apple presents itself in the light and shadow, planes and lines of his painting.

Both the odour of the fruits and the museum's waxed wooden floors fill my hour in Basel. And, even as I leave, Cézanne's colours and lines continue to transform my perceptions. Space becomes an event, a genesis. I walk toward the cathedral, my eyes construct and deconstruct the well-kept patrician dwellings. I read their façades according to modulations of colour and shape. The light of the sky lends breath to the city and to the still life I've just studied.

All his life Cézanne persevered, painted humble things, and did not listen to his father's admonition: "My son, think of the future. You die by being a genius, and you eat by having money." Ninety-five years later, *Still Life with Apples and Peaches* continues to unravel its own narratives. Rooted in the soil of Provence, it now illuminates the north. On a Sunday afternoon in spring, I don't head directly back to my quotidian life. I remain a silent lover of fruits and vases, of pitchers and wooden tables.

## Table

I often stand early spring days
before Cézanne's *Still Life with Apples and Peaches*
to lean on its wooden table,
the fruits' sharp tang under
my tongue, the surprise he brought
to Paris with an apple; and as I bend down
touching sun on smooth skins, the blond table
shows its baroquely cut apron,
as salesladies did when I was young,
tabliers or smocks,
old-fashioned garments of sturdy cloth,
which I wash, iron and mend
on the gleaming, honey-brown silence
of Cézanne's kitchen table early Spring days.

### In Cézanne's studio, we're dappled with joy

On a dish recline the peaches. Brilliant yellow, burnt
  vermillion
and green earth his palette, silence in the high room.

Always they face him, waiting. He thinks light, paints
a dark cleft. Such soft cheeks. Their curves.

Like a bed the white cloth under them. Bright, silky, it
  rises
and falls before him, slides from the smooth table down
  canvas.

He opens sweet flesh. Strange glamour,
lush nakedness gazing up. Before the rich brocade
  curtain,

the gleaming jug. He bends over their serious faces,
discards the brush.

## Chardin's Alphabet of Things

I travel into Chardin's works and hear their voices in the sound box of imagination by way of an exhibition catalogue. On winter evenings, near our living room fire, freed from the shuffle of museum visitations and the cultural bustle that obscures art works, I participate fully in Chardin's world, feel the visceral power of his still lifes. A lover rather than a tourist, I watch the paintings opening up like loaves of bread in a warm oven. The canvases seem filled with utensils from my parents' home: simple coffee pots, glasses, knives, baskets of fruit return me to the days, rooms, light of my childhood.

In my youth, still lifes didn't much appeal to me. Compared to landscapes and portraits by renowned Dutch artists, portrayals of household utensils, vegetables and animals seemed ordinary, too familiar. Unknowingly I was practising the 18th century ranking of genres, placing still lifes at the bottom of artistic achievements. In middle age, familiar now with Cézanne's still lifes and knowing his admiration for Chardin, I came to realize that the representation of quotidian things can sanctify the everyday. At present, the more I examine still lifes, the more I stand in awe before them and the artists who practice the cataloguing impulse of Whitman's *Leaves of Grass* or such Latin canticles as *Benedicite, omnia opera domini*. And I want to respond to their record of what is closest to us, of what resonates with our basic daily rounds, with the seemingly intimate permutations that occur there.

Diderot called Chardin "a great magician with mute compositions," and Cézanne referred to him as a "crafty devil." What do we know of this man whose last self-portrait pictures the artist working at his easel? Born in Paris in 1699, he had hardly ever left that city when he died there in 1779. A member of the Royal Academy of the Arts, granted lodgings in the Louvre, and a pension from the king, Chardin was not an artist whose works intended to herald the political changes to come. Nor did he conform to the expectations of the day, which demanded that artists paint historical or mythological subjects. His uneventful life, as well as his tranquil art, unfolded independently of both sides in the social turmoil and inequalities which climaxed in the French Revolution less than a decade after his death.

Raised in a working bourgeois milieu — his father, a Parisian cabinetmaker specializing in billiard tables, was cabinetmaker to the king — Chardin was constant in character and led a well-ordered Parisian middle-class existence. During a time of extreme social injustice and upheaval, he elected to paint simple images from everyday life. He ignored the frivolous games of the aristocrats, the coquettish Watteauian dances of elegant cavaliers with shepherdesses in the woods. Without conspicuous painterly verbiage, he told the story, painted a history of things as we already know them — or rather, as we forget them. His canvases portray the neat, rhythmic gestures, the unsung duties and virtues of humble folk, surrounding their alertness and unaffected naturalness with a softness and joy.

What guarantees that scenes of quotidian tranquility do not merely mask domestic mediocrity? How do straightforward, low-key paintings seemingly devoid of psychological complexities work? How are we to approach these images? How much do they allow us into their game? Chardin's genre scene *The Schoolmistress* gives us a hint. Here a young girl instructs a child in the alphabet. Innocently transfixed, this small pupil is absorbed by the signs on the page: He still has all to learn. Absorbed in Chardin's art, we re-enact that child's watchfulness, hold our breath while our attention is first mobilized, then led into contemplation. We learn the alphabet and the peace of simple things. Late in his life Rilke reiterated this lesson in *The Duino Elegies*: "Are we perhaps here merely to say house, bridge, fountain, gate, jug, fruit-tree, window, / Or column, or tower . . . "

Chardin's roll call of plates, glasses, baskets, crockery, knives and fruits from the family of everyday things pulls us out of our insensibility into their physicality. The paintings rescue these seemingly trivial things from the no-man's land of oblivious use, restore them to their own coherence. Marcel Proust wrote: "We have learned from Chardin that a pear is as alive as a woman, that an ordinary piece of pottery is as beautiful as a precious stone."

What do we discover then when we explore the early *Basket of Plums, Bottle, Glass of Water and Cucumbers* (1728)? Only a stone shelf on which lush, velvety blue plums, two cool yellow large cucumbers flank a charcoal-coloured bottle and a translucent half-filled glass of water? Or consider the inventory of *Carafe of Wine, Silver Goblet, Five Cherries, Two Peaches, an Apricot and a Green Apple* (1728): Is there anything here besides the shine of a Prussian blue goblet which reflects the red fruits and is overtowered by the dark sparkle of a half-filled wine bottle jutting out of the dark background? The weight, consistency and volume of each item in these two works are so intensely observed that, driven by an insatiable appetite, we spontaneously move to grab them. In these earthy utensils and fruits dailiness is rescued, and we learn a lesson of things.

With even greater subtlety, these still lifes move beyond that initial lesson. *The Glass of Water and Coffee Pot* (1760), a marvel with its gleaming glazed brown pot, the still water in the glass and the three white garlic heads, incites the viewer to harken to what Baudelaire called in his poem "Élévation" the silence of "mute things" — beyond light and texture. A similar quiet eloquence fascinates in *Basket of Plums with Walnuts, Currants and Cherries* (1765), where the silken, violet skins of the plums and the subdued cherries are cast against a warm brown background and rest on an ochre ledge. With the basket's reddish-brown tints, they form a soothing harmony. We hear a melody antithetical to the din of confused daily existence.

*Basket of Wild Strawberries* (1761) is another late composition of warm reds, browns and ochre yellows. Strawberries rise pyramid-like up into a subdued chocolate background, while a faceted glass, two white carnations, a peach and two cherries bathe in a chiaroscuro of shapes and shadows. A glow leads the eye from seen to unseen. Chardin's brush illuminates his subjects from within; they take on a life of their own and the perceiver recedes. The canvases enact what can happen in old age: rather than grabbing and consuming the things before us, we contemplate them with tender relinquishment. Summoned from their darkness, Chardin's inanimate protagonists then welcome us, for an elusive moment, into their inscrutable mystery.

This lesson of old age plays also in Chardin's scenes from after the hunt. In the early paintings such as *Hare with Game Bag and Powder Flask* (1730), the dead animals are boldly laid out centre stage. In the later representations, such as *A Rabbit, Two Thrushes and Some Straw on a Stone Table* (1755), where the colour tones are compassionate, warmer, the animals occupy a less predominant place, are surrounded by empty space. Their pelts and feathers are not realistically painted, they lie abandoned in death. No longer provocative in their silence, their youthful aggressiveness vanished, these depictions of inarticulate beasts affirm the entire span of life and death.

At the end of his life, his still lifes no longer appreciated, Chardin fell into disgrace with the Academy; his son drowned in a Venetian canal and his eyes were paralyzed by his use of oil paints. Undaunted by these defeats, Chardin espoused with self-confidence a new technique for new subjects: he painted portraits in pastel. During his last seven years he surprised his public with three extraordinary self-portraits. Of these, *Chardin at his Easel* (1779) is a masterful study of an elderly artist preparing for death. Wrinkled and thin, this disorderly old man looks at us with a curious, intent gaze, beyond the gleam of his steel spectacles. In contrast to the decline of competence we generally expect of old age, his vigorous fingers raise the weapon of his trade, a red pastel crayon, in salute. Chardin paints here a paean of praise to old age, his last instruction to us.

During the long winter evenings, Chardin's still lifes stimulate my sensorial memory. I relish them each night in liturgical fashion, and I remember Whitman's saying: "The Insignificant is as big to me as any." And I come to understand why these striking images have survived until today: They embody the transient richness of typical things from everyday experience, and transmit the least intrusive moments of learning in our lives.

**Chardin before the Easel**

Undaunted and alert, agile as a lizard,
at his easel with steel-rimmed pince-nez,
measuring our thoughts, intently,
the sum of his seventy years.  He's determined
not to lose his art, gave up oils,
for the veils pastels hang over faces.
Two dim embers still warm, his eyes
a single-minded silence,
open the locks of goblets, plates, fruits,
spar with well-ordered, quotidian gods.
"Yes I'm worn out," he says, the crafty devil, stirring so
that in his wrinkled face the sun rises.
And returns for exhibitions about every twenty years:
alive amidst his inanimate, mute things.

## FENCING WITH THE IMPOSSIBLE

We're standing on a narrow street in the heart of Rouen, the capital of Normandy, peering up at the sky. The sun bathes the old dwellings. No sound, the smell of coffee and baking bread. Before us the cathedral slices the heavens, but instead I see Monet's paintings engraved on my mind. The way the stones waver and the portals trap light, the way the entire façade appears and evaporates like an immense vertical lake. Behind this Gothic monolith, I sense what preoccupied Monet from February 1892 until April 1893, what he called his duel with "the impossible" — his attempts to depict a monument of extraordinary splendour, constructed by divinely-inspired architects and stonemasons, grounded in both art and nature.

This afternoon sunlight quivers on the roofs of Rouen, plays off the  belfries of the sanctuary's west portal. These golden stones gave birth to Monet's paintings. All around us the little stores and medieval houses facing the *place de la cathédrale* come alive; at once solid and light the church soars up as though a wonder of nature. In my studies of Monet's works, I dwell upon the blues and pinks of early morning, the oranges and whites of midday heat, the mauves and browns of evening, all brushing over the façade. However, I also relive a mundane incident at the corner of the *rue Ampère*, one of the three locations where Monet executed his work. Here the artist faced eviction from Mr. Lévy's *Boutique de lingerie et modes* because the ladies of Rouen refused to try on clothes while a bearded man painted near the window. The shopkeeper tolerated the painter on his premises only after being paid a tripled daily rent.

Next day in the Rouen Museum, I examine closely the sole painting of Monet's series which remains here, one of thirty. He built up the surface of the canvas with encrusted layers of paint, simulating the masonry of a medieval church, and transfiguring a stone mass into another masterpiece. The superimposed colours reflect the poetry of the stones as sunrise turns them to lemon yellows, as fog veils them with blues, as late morning softens them to pinks, as noon sun reverberates on them, and evening rain shrouds them in cobalt and purple.

This one view of the cathedral calls to mind Monet's two-year struggle. His letters to his wife document his meticulous daily routines:

> I am worn out. I have never been so exhausted physically and morally; it has driven me silly and I only want my bed... Imagine that I get up before 6:00 a.m. and work from 7:00 a.m. until 6:30 in the evening, always standing.

Nor in bed could he shake his labours: "I slept a night filled with nightmares: The Cathedral would crash on top of me, it would appear either blue or pink or yellow." His thumb swollen from holding the palette, constantly assailed by doubts, he felt himself a prisoner of the holy shrine. Even though, during his lifetime, he produced more than 500 drawings, 2000 paintings and 3100 letters, at a moment of discouragement he wrote his wife:

> They are not very farsighted, those who see a master in

me! Beautiful intentions, yes, but that's it! Happy the
younger ones, those who believe that it is easy; I was like
that once, but it's over; yet tomorrow morning at 7:00
I'll be there again.

Each day his enthusiasm overcame depression, anxieties and
self-deprecation, and drove him to besiege his model anew, in
solitude and concentration. His resolve did not flag. Seldom
did he go home to Giverny on weekends; he even discouraged
his wife from visiting until he had finished the thirty can-
vases. On them the real cathedral converses with the painted
one, reality reveals itself evanescently in a marriage with art.

Our visit to Rouen, where stones and paintings
intermingle, occasions a better encounter with the artist than
a grand exposition of all his works. The road beckons toward
the provinces, Monet's gardens with their water lilies. We
drive toward them now, beside the Seine, the vermillions of
the cathedral still on our eyes.

I had always wanted to visit Giverny, a modest village
between Paris and Rouen. Monet moved there in 1883 and
remained there until his death in 1926. He bought a large
property adjacent to the railroad tracks, where trains steamed
by four times each day. Later, when Monet purchased
another parcel of land, the train line ran through the estate
itself. Monet created a garden paradise around the tracks,
after fighting the residents of Giverny for permission to divert
the waters of the Epte River to refresh his water lily pond.
That task successfully accomplished, he painted over 250
paintings of his flower and water garden, some of them
monumental.

Today Giverny is the second most visited site of France;

thousands of pilgrims step over its ground, perhaps believing that "the garden is the man." Luckily, on this cool June morning, we are a small group moving first through the traditional Western flower garden, laid out formally like the park of a country house, then entering a silent, meditative place, the Eastern water lily garden, fashioned more naturally with its Japanese bridge, fruit trees, bamboo, weeping willows and pond. With their mix of Eastern and Western plantings, the two gardens complement one another in a joint celebration of the multipliciy of natural beauty.

Relying on a team of six full-time gardeners, Monet diligently orchestrated the changing terrain which stood model for all his later paintings. So enwrapped did he become in his landscape of earth and water, he often employed horticultural metaphors when referring to his painting: *"Je pioche,"* he would say to his friends, "I'm hoeing, opening new ground." To get the light to dart in and out, to make the plants quiver on his canvas, required the same handiwork and vision as working the earth with hand and spade. Like Cézanne, who venerated Mont Sainte-Victoire for twenty years, Monet focused on this garden for the last two decades of his life, celebrating the power of natural growth. Whereas Cézanne was driven toward the majesty of rocky upsurges, Monet stood galvanized before the innocence of a water-lily growth, and humbly offered it his technical prowess as a gift rather than a form of mastery. In accordance, every fall the gardeners removed the water lilies from the pond into greenhouses for the winter months.

As I walk through the garden, where perhaps the painter-gardener's easel had once been positioned on a bright June day like this one, I am seized by the same amazement I experienced some years ago before Cézanne's mountain. What lovers of solitude and privacy both men must have been that they would leave the roiling urban, political scene of Paris behind for spacious nature. As for Monet, he evidently found reassurance in the restfully exotic carpets of water lilies. They float serenely on the pond, merge into the dense growth of multicoloured reflections cast on the water by the surrounding foliage. At first, in his late canvases, a bridge still alerts us to a human presence, then humans disappear entirely, nature speaks in her own terms, timeless and secluded.

As the garden greets us, Monet's vision sharpens our senses to the multiple relations of these natural surroundings. Simultaneously I return to my first acquaintance with Monet's huge *Water Lily Panels* at the Paris Orangerie in 1961. The Orangerie *Water Lilies* are expansive like a symphony. The light refracts a lurking depth, their eerie calm and pearliness brim with a feast of colours. They are seductive, mysterious, dream-like. That space appeared to me a glorious haven of an artist's dogged endurance against threatening blindness, bore witness to the subterranean pulsations of nature. Then, almost forty years ago, I vowed to seek out the Giverny garden.

Reproductions of Monet's flowers shine on the walls of our bedroom; they hang there as delivery from academic ordinariness. Their incantatory affirmation of simple things keeps my faith buoyant, makes me live within their certainty and tenderness. Baudelaire had longed "to understand without effort the language of flowers and mute things"; Rimbaud's prose poems attempted to free elemental forces of nature from the distorting human eye. Monet's uncharted course in landscape painting parallels those quests.  The restricted site of Giverny spawned the most daringly mysterious and elusive paintings of the twentieth century.  Here in this lush cult garden, I don't merely exchange complicitous glances with a dead artist who moved with the bravura and grace of a great cat, I espouse his vision — a vision that eternalizes what we tend to forget.  I learn that gardens, paintings and poems respond, if entered and loved.  The garden still dazzles and refreshes us while we stroll through the adjacent cemetery. The artist's simple tomb, as well as his words "we must help one another to see things better," exude his unflagging love of the land.  I'm ready to go work.

## Education

> *School was always like a prison to me,*
> *I could never bring myself to stay there,*
> *even four hours a day...*
>
> Claude Monet

It barred him from the sea lovestruck
by the sun.  Leisurely mists latticing
cliffs and shallows
turned his eye into a palace.
He did believe in learning;
later, intense studies harnessed his fingers,
his thoughts, as he composed with colours
hymns of light, waterlilies, ponds,
their intoxicating phantasies, their wild
shadows, desirable as a schoolroom's empty
blackboard, widening like a lover's mouth.

**Some hundred years later**
**outside the Cathedral of Rouen**
**Monet's canvases unlock our life**

They name the hour's pungent spice

Vertical light reaching down
a caress of fire

God in that luminous monolith,

air turned to gem
stone vaporized to cloud.

**Claude Monet's Water Landscapes**

They were his victory in old age,
seductive as Venus — strong, invisible legs,
waterlily clusters pearly pink, then
mauve. They looked
at him, women in silk underclothes,
the rushing flames of alcove and bed.
Clouds trailed new light
over their faces. Even asleep, his eyes held
to their blooms. Soft rain and winds
tinged his pleasure. Waterbound muses of deep
promise, each day
they rose from the mirror
of desire, as his garden grew
ripe. No swaying or sweeping
or unlit swirls through midnight fields
disturbed their tête-à-tête.

# III

# Switzerland:

# Venerators of Rock

## Sunday Mood of the Heart

"The sun brings a Sunday mood into the heart," Giovanni Giacometti wrote to Richard Buehler in 1910. And, indeed, his life and art were a constant struggle for light. As an inhabitant of Bregaglia, a remote Swiss valley flanked on its south side with a high mountain range, he waited impatiently each February for the sun to return from its three month absence. After one such darkness, he exclaimed in a letter: "... what life there is in the sunrays ... at the moment when the sun comes again golden, rich and warm over the mountains and floods my atelier, there is jubilation in the entire house." His art is a clarion call, gives voice to the light of his native place. However, Giovanni Giacometti did not merely celebrate light as a metaphor in colour and word; he sought to experience it directly and to penetrate the sun itself. Toward this aim he held nothing back, threw his body and soul at the heavenly target.

Giacometti was a remarkable correspondent. In the hundreds of letters he wrote, he revealed himself a self-taught philosopher with a clear vision of the thrust of his life and painting. These letters disclose the intensity of his love for his native valley: "... a good star, the love of my art and my home valley guided me ... This small piece of land, surrounded by mountains, is for me the world. Here I was born, here my imagination took flight, here my eyes perceived for the first time the light." They manifest the recuperative force of his art: "Paintbrush and colours are the faithful interpreters of my thoughts, my dreams, my life." And they reveal how deeply he dreamed of capturing the light: "What runs through my work, is a vision of light, my childhood dream... The struggle for light is the main spring of my work."

Who is this passionate advocate of land and light? Along with Giovanni Segantini and Ferdinand Hodler, he was one of the great Swiss mountain depicters of the last century. Father of the celebrated sculptor and painter, Alberto Giacometti, Giovanni and his achievements have been overshadowed by the son's fame. I too came only to him via his son. However, soon after I began to visit the Bregaglia Valley and started to study his art, I discovered that Alberto Giacometti would have never become a renowned artist had he not been encouraged by his father. That father was an exuberant visionary of self-reliance who loved what was wild and free. He valued "above all else independence." For that reason, after he had lived and studied in his youth in Paris and Munich, he returned home. There surrounded by his family — his wife Annetta, the anchor for his art, and his four children, his constant models — his Dionysian heart and creative energies could unfold without the detractions of larger art centres. His son Bruno relates that even after his father had achieved fame, he remained closely allied to the peasants of his village Stampa. In the local inn he would talk and play cards with them on winter evenings, and during the spring months he joined them outside to play bocca, a practice continued by his son Alberto during his yearly stays at home. Before sending his paintings off for exhibitions in cities, he held a show in his atelier for the village peasants. According to Bruno, he wanted to show them that, while they cultivated the fields, he too worked.

Giovanni Giacometti was an avid, creative reader, not only of books, but also of his mountainous terrain. He registered there the smallest details until they became the text and commentary of his life: "Every day the mysterious play of life and the infinite beauty of nature renew themselves before my eyes." He never tired of combing the outdoors for motifs. His life is the story of a man who painted to think and feel ecstatically: "My life is my art, my art is my life." He virtually devoured the valley, sky, torrents and peaks, exulting in their tang, in their rocky, light-drenched tones, until his art became an earthly prayer. Never having deserted his native valley, he gained a tranquility of heart and a constant terrain of inspiration, a seedbed for his rhapsodies. A sacred sense of vocation and a powerful commitment inform all his activities: "Like a Vestal Virgin, I try to preserve the flame that benevolent nature put into my heart, and I try to light and heat my work with it." Up to his last breath he did not cease to test his impulses against the clarities of the alpine world, perfecting a transparent style. He had his Sabbath when the light danced and rang out in his paintings.

Early in my acquaintance with Giovanni Giacometti, *Self-Portrait before a Winter Landscape* (1899) arrested me: In the foreground the artist's upper torso comes toward us, while the background is closed off by a steep mountain chain. Alpine houses seem to rest on one of the figure's broad shoulders; in the distance, on the valley floor, below the peaks, a funeral procession winds its way toward a church steeple. In sharp contrast to the predominantly white snowy landscape, the warm reds and greens of the human figure draw our attention to his face. The brown cap, which covers hair and forehead, as well as his upturned red mustache point toward large blue eyes. Their curious, open gaze fixes us with utmost concentration. These eyes set out to wrestle with the heavenly fire.

The sun's rays appear for the first time in *Sunrise* (1912). The sky occupies here the upper third of the canvas. Rising beyond the lake, mountains recede behind a veil of light beams. Though not directly visible, the sun transforms the landscape — the mountains into purple castles and the lake into a gleaming mirror of green and gold. All shades and shapes seem saturated in invisible sunlight.

Eight years later, in *Lark* (1920), the upper two thirds of the canvas are given over to the heavens. There sunrays dart through an outer ring of clouds, surrounding a central blue funnel-like space. We are drawn into a cosmic heavenly event. The rising green meadows of the high mountain plateau form the lower third of the image; they seem bewitched, drawn upward into the circular rotation on the sky's vault. No human habitation or activity is present to receive the crown of solar rays which strike landscape and viewer.

Finally in 1926, Giacometti achieved what Cézanne had deemed impossible. *Winter Sun near Maloja* portrays not only the light beams, but the sun itself. We experience this time the immediate solar ball above an alpine landscape in the dead of winter. The crystalline, blue sky on the upper two thirds of the canvas becomes the stage for the sun's glittering reign. The light drenches, almost obliterates, the snow-covered land on the lower third of the painting. The earth's snowy surface dissolves under lacy pink. Everything appears to sacrifice its individual substance to light. In this apotheosis of the sun, only the full glory of manifestation counts.

Whereas Alberto Giacometti admired the soft, delicate colours of Fra Angelico and instantiated a faintly muted and distant light on his canvases, Giovanni was heir to the rich, luminous tones of Van Gogh. He sank himself deeply into Van Gogh's letters: "I like no book as much as this one." Consequently, his diction and colours were burningly expansive, his landscapes lit by an insomniac light, an illumination present even when unseen. Everything in his art utters the strong word: *sun, Sonne, sole*. Not merely satisfied with the intoxicating first kiss of February sun, when the Bregaglia Valley woke out of the shadows, Giovanni Giacometti, like Prometheus, wanted to steal the heavenly fire; in paintings like *Winter Sun near Maloja* he succeeds.

We're not surprised to learn that Giovanni's passionate celebration of light in colour and word came with an extraordinary plenitude of heart. As the years went by his very person radiated the light of his beloved alpine peaks. Wherever he appeared he ignited cheerfulness. Upon his death in 1933, Daniel Baud-Bovy's eulogy underlined this; "Dear, charming Giovanni," he said, "it's almost inconceivable that we shall no more see the gleaming face onto which the sun of inspiration cast its beams."

After he had visited the 1907 Cézanne exposition in Paris this man, who naturally illuminated his surroundings, wrote to his friend the art collector Hédy Hahnloser-Buehler: "Great works refresh the courage and renew the hope that perhaps one doesn't live in vain and that one sacrifices oneself for a noble cause." His lifelong devotion to art and land was blessed and rewarded; Giovanni Giacometti's very person became ecstatic. He is ultimately a painter of affirmation; his enterprise was joyous and redemptive. He painted the forever startling and freshening power of the world. And so I see him ahead of me on an alpine path, urging me to be creative, to always risk more, to give my best self, and to ascend with him on that mountain into the sun.

### Giovanni Giacometti's Self-Portrait, 1899

The sun looks at me, artist's eye in a winter landscape.
Open-gazed, curious. It's my star,
all brilliance and home.

There are no funerals, no avalanches.
Some skies are veiled, some
glamorous. I paint the solar voice
like an oratorio, hear
my wife and children next door.

I soar, playing in the conservatory of light,
when my family laughs, and joins me.

## A VISIONARY OF SPACE

One winter night in Canada I dreamed I was walking with Alberto Giacometti, walking through his native Val Bregaglia, the narrow Swiss Valley that runs from Maloja into Italy a few kilometres away. Three-thousand-metre peaks line both sides — verdant, wooded slopes to the north, stark, crystalline granite to the south. Giacometti felt at home in the village of Stampa crouched low on the valley floor. His listening and talking in the little street, an extended conversation between the peaks and the valley. In my dream his words leaned toward celebration and transcendence, he invoked Nietzsche who had lived seven successive summers up valley in Sils Maria at the end of the 19th century. In our verbal exchange my own re-writing echoed his process for remodelling his creations. Don't I do with words what he did with clay and paint? His strategies and ideas reverberate in my working habits; his reveries and meditations are mine.

The following spring, I walked with my companion through the Giacometti retrospective exhibition in the Zurich Kunsthaus, a collection of ninety statues, forty paintings and sixty drawings. The towering granite of the Val Bregaglia, its jagged summits, soared through the sculptures on show. In their rough, broken surfaces the menace and sublimity of that rocky territory became palpable again. They flickered, seemed ready to move, inspired at once intimacy and awe. Luminous blocks carved in space, homages to life, these uncanny statues embodied Nietzsche's exclamation: "Art is essential affirmation, benediction, deification of existence."

I kept asking what was so special about Giacometti's statues? Other artists, both painters and sculptors, peopled the 20th century with their creations. Yet, judging from the prolific literature about his work, it seems that Giacometti remains a startling figure, and somehow revolutionized our way to live space. Still how can we enter the seductive, persuasive language with which his statues operate on us?

The elongated female figures stand motionless; they could be slender dancers at rest. Their male counterparts, fugitive, walking or pointing might be denuded trees from a petrified forest come unexpectedly alive. Are they boulders come down from the mountains? Archaic deities? Athletic saints? Whatever their status, they pull us out from our blunted routines. We look at them intently, as though from the distant past; out of instinctive memory, a forgotten delight comes back — our first erect standing, proud walking unaided across a room. Now grown up, we sense only dimly how it was, then, to feel our feet and arms amazed and moving. On one level, Giacometti's statues take us to that memorable place of childhood wonder. They dramatize powerfully that event so that we fall in love again with movements, that particular joy. After a lifetime of unconscious peregrinations, our imaginations are seized by the grammar of simple gestures. The fragile, mysterious figures catch and inscribe humans in space — and in time, reaching both backward and forward. They teach us something about the experience of stillness and motion. Here in Zurich I understood the full power of Nietzsche's phrase, "Art teaches us to have delight in existence."

But Giacometti is a conjurer of another kind, one who

urges the viewer to cross a threshold and move beyond fond recollections of elemental gestures; his statues mediate a compound experience. While creating something new, they restore something ancient and archaic. These art works sing with a mysterious spiritual tonality in their 20th century language. Somehow they have us cross into a timeless realm. If we stand long enough before them, their evanescence comes to inhabit us like a prayer, like release.

How does this compression and expansion work, and where does it lead us? Within the dark exterior of the figures sparkles an eternal radiance. This distant star-like brilliance seems to come from beyond, asks us to let go everything associated with ordinary, artistic depiction until a clarifying experience occurs. It is as though something sacred dwelled here — another authority, taking from us the burden of the day and inciting us to a free flight, a soaring emergence. We're silent in our gazing. The innocent majesty of that authority inspires awe, and we remember Nietzsche's call to be swept back into life through art: "To live we need at every moment art... We have art so that we won't be destroyed by truth."

Early the second morning of our visit to Zurich, before crowds had filled the museum, I followed Giacometti's men and women in their walk beyond language. They came to life again, became maps to the earth's sanctuary. Epiphanic instances of human longing for the sacred, they point to that terrain, are touchstones of consolation. Indeed they haunt us with the thought that revelation awaits us everywhere if only we can say "Yes" to reality: "Art teaches us to love life, to look at life in all its forms with interest and love... and to say at last: 'However life may be, it is good'."

The ideal way to take in the alchemy of the sacred in

Giacometti's works is not to dream of walking with him through his native valley but to be a solitary actor in the theatre of his moving men and women. Then later, the performance over, we go backstage into our own world transformed. Within that private sanctum, we recapture the intense bliss of having communed with the children of a visionary of space. We can welcome Giacometti's totemic witnesses and pursuers back into our lives. Perhaps they could keep us company forever. Perhaps we could summon with them the ineffable.

### Terra Firma

*Alberto Giacometti Retrospective, Zurich 2001*

With Giacometti, you move amidst walking statues,
suspecting they might stride on
when you leave the exhibition, return,
humbly, en masse,
to the mountain.  They know
everything about rock,
and its genius.  You are not
in a museum, but strolling
straight into the country of the heart.
Step up to
Giacometti's paintings,
into his mother's huge wood-panelled eyes:
a terra cotta nostalgia,
where you talk, eat,
read, near the side of an earthy
goddess.  A serenity
holds you, the stone's
last flare at sundown.  Terra firma,
not a narrow crest over
void, a path to take, to start
breathing, building, dwelling.
                              With Giacometti.
To walk into purer tints and lines,
gestures, always effaced.

**The Cat**

At night, when cafés open their doors
and Giacometti leaves his brush,
the cat pulls on its boots,
struts out to join
the vagabonds in their vesperal rites.

And Giacometti, intent
over a café table, thinks
of destroying a Rembrandt
at the Louvre
to free a trapped cat, or
of saving without hesitation
the cat
should his atelier burn down . . .

### 46, rue Hippolyte-Maindron

At dawn outside the
workshop, a thrush in the tree
sings, tuning the scuptor's ear
with salvos of joy.

The leaves are a concert hall for that musician,
always the sky lit yellow,
Paris posing as jungle, wet
mud to be shaped.

Always
Giacometti alone with the bird
*I don't know who I am nor what I'm doing*
*... and those matchsticks dispersed*
*battleships on a grey ocean*
he writes.

# IV

## ITALY:

## SAINTS AND HENCHMEN

WINDOWS OPEN ONTO THE INFINITE

To be happy in Italy, we go to Bergamo's old town, the semi-forgotten Sleeping Beauty high on a hill at the foot of the Alps. On its Piazza Vecchia, at the terrace of the Caffè Tasso, we spend a balmy spring hour sipping cappuccino. While we study the young men and women flirting on the square, the sights visited that morning play over our memory: the polychrome marble façade of the Colleoni Chapel; the Santa Maria Maggiore Basilica where Lorenzo Lotto created the choir intarsias of Old Testament stories inlaid in wood and overlaid by Christian and alchemical symbols; the high, covered stairway of the Palazzo della Ragione with its view of red roofs and cupolas rising toward heaven; the house of Donizetti, father of the *bel canto*. And always walking slowly over egg-sized pebbles encased in the cement of the narrow streets with brightly lit stores and boutiques on the ground floor of high old aristocratic dwellings. Then we emerge on the fortified parapets amidst lovers lounging on benches, and finally we enter a small, packed church in time for a wedding.

That evening we participate in a Renaissance dream, as we enjoy the Italian cuisine at Da Vittorio's in the lower city. In that very elegant gourmet restaurant, the Mama and Papa, formally attired, pitch in as their sons serve the guests. Our activities of the day in the old city perched above the wooded, bucolic terraces and accessible by the quaint 19th century funicular, still reverberate in our heads while blasts of fireworks and trumpets enter from the street outside. The

youths of Bergamo are celebrating Italy's victory in the 8th
Final of the World Soccer Cup.  The police have blocked off
the streets for that wild outdoor display.  Over dessert we
anticipate tomorrow's visits to the Bergamo churches with
Lorenzo Lotto's altar paintings, and to the Accademia Carrara
which is hosting the exhibition *Lorenzo Lotto, the Restless
Genius of the Renaissance.*

   Who is Lorenzo Lotto?  Fed on the art of his more
celebrated colleagues Titian, Bellini and Raphael, I had not
heard of him before the spring of 1998.  Born in Venice in
1480, he was a non-conformist, peripatetic artist who
wouldn't let himself be strapped into the conventions and
intrigues endured by his more ambitious peers.  Unmarried,
he travelled restlessly from place to place, dwelling to
dwelling, accepting commissions in Venice, Rome, Bergamo
and the Marches.  In 1549, seven years before his death, tired
and sick, he moved for good to the Marches, a province far
removed from the cultural centres.  He joined the religious
community of the Basilica of Loretto as an oblate, and ended
his earthly existence in tranquil contemplation.  Often mis-
understood, Lotto was even suspected of being a Protestant
sympathizer, because he painted two portraits of Luther and
his wife.

   The agitation of his frequent transplantations lends his art
its distinctive individuality:   bright colours and moving
figures.  His religious scenes, both mystic and softly intimate,
are marked by a consoling sweetness.  The grave serenity and
dramatic intensity of his portraits exude an aura of icons.
With their luminous and limpid spirituality, his paintings
reconcile the world with heavenly spheres.  Here in Bergamo,
where Lotto painted many of them, the works on exhibit are

firmly planted in their home ground.  In the darkened rooms of the Accademia Carrara their radiance is an overwhelming source of light.  On this hot June day, as if alive, they eavesdropped with pleasure on the Italian conversations around them.

In Lotto's altar pieces athletic angels soar through heaven with Bach's partitas; in his portraits, baroque music seems constantly to play in the sitters' heads.  Lotto, a genius of the portrait, did as much for that genre as Baudelaire did for French love poetry.  The earliest portrait in this exhibit is the 1505 *Bishop Bernardo de Rossi*.  A high ecclesiastic official — fist clenched around a scroll — stands before the bright green curtain which frames his head; the folds angled toward his face focus attention on his light, cold eyes.  The bishop's authoritative presence reveals his resolute combativeness in his conflicts with the leaders of Treviso, a town where he instituted reforms.  From his intent, steely gaze we can surmise he had the required strength to evade the attempts on his life.  In *Portrait of a Lady* from the same period, the light, falling from the left side rather than from above, enlivens also the frank stare of this corpulent, stolid matron with the finesse of incandescence.  Unidealized, turned full face, her detached eyes seek us out uncannily.

No less astonishing and full of bravado is the dramatic close-up *Judith with the Head of Holofernes* (1512).  This little miniature depicts the perpetrators of the bloody crime emerging from shadowy night:  the young widow Judith, a Rubenesque blond, puts the decapitated head of the enemy general into the sack held by her maid servant.  Judith heroically brandishes Holofernes' sword with which she accomplished the gruesome deed.  The bright blue, red, yellow, white and green colours of the two women's dresses, the pearls on Judith's tight bodice, her dangling pearl earrings, render her especially seductive.  But it is the determined look on her fine aristocratic face, contrasting the bewildered expression, upturned nose and brutish features of the maid, which captures the viewer.

While he was staying in Bergamo, Lotto's art reached a peak.  The portrait of *Lucina Brembati* (1518), with a dramatic interaction between what is seen and what is absent, is one instance of his balanced compositions.  Lotto here casts the female sitter unconventionally in the style reserved for males, before a large, red velvet curtain.  Dressed  in an expensive damask dress, an embroidered shirt-waist, a large headdress strung with pearls, and several gold and pearl necklaces, this noblewoman displays her social status confidently.  Yet the nocturnal setting and the pale moon in the sky point to something concealed, something to be discovered.

Around 1523 Lotto also finished two of the most startling portraits of married couples in Italian painting.  In these two conjugal portraits of Bergamo patrons, the searching gaze of the sitters seek us out as though awaiting a response.  Lotto was indeed a portraitist with a feeling for narratives:  the vivacity and sudden shafts of light in these images invite us to invent complex relations within their social contexts.  In *Marsilio Casotti and his Bride Faustina* the clever eyes of the woman and the dark ones of the man pierce beyond us into the future.  We witness the betrothal of a couple in ornate headgear and bejewelled clothes: the groom is about to place a ring on his bride's finger, as a mischievous Cupid lowers onto their shoulders a yoke with budding laurel leaves, reminding them of their marital duties as well as of the virtues of chastity and fidelity.

Not the depiction of a wedding, but rather a celebration of conjugal fidelity, *Portrait of a Married Couple* tells a different story. On the arm of a lady sits a dog, on the table sleeps a squirrel to which the man points as he holds a paper inscribed "Man Never," and behind the sitters a window opens onto a wind-blown landscape. The painting suggests a mood of loyal friendship and mutual support. The woman, positioned higher and more prominently than the man, places a hand onto his shoulder. The couple's expressive, large black eyes remind me of Etruscan statues. Her fixed stare and pallor intimate an other-worldliness, while the man's strong gaze indicates a personage resolute and faithful. An inventive white brushstroke films his eyes with tears, his red eyelids and nose indicate pain. Research has revealed that Lotto painted this portrait after the death of the man's wife. An inconsolable widower, unlike the squirrel that sleeps during a storm, he remembers the acute torments of his life.

Lotto's Bergamo portraits are buoyant; life rushes through them in brilliant colours and quick movements. The later portraits, executed in Venice and the Marches, are less joyful and more reflective. Lotto painted them after disappointments and tiring peregrinations. A possible exception here is the 1533 *Portrait of a Lady as Lucretia*. In a magnificent orange and green striped silk dress with fur trim, a lady faces us with provocative, confrontational stare and strong sweeping gesture. On her breast a sumptuously large ruby with pendant pearl framed by gold putti is suspended from several strands of gold chain. In her left hand she holds a drawing representing the Roman heroine Lucretia, who having been raped, committed suicide, preferring death to dishonour for herself and her husband. The right hand of the sitter points to a paper on the table inscribed: "Nor shall any unchaste woman live through the example of Lucretia." The frank, outward gaze of Lotto's lady, her explicit way of drawing attention to the two pieces of paper, suggest that she wishes to remain chaste and abide by marital virtue.

Who cannot but be moved by the forcefully direct dark eyes in *Fra Gregorio Belo* (1547), the friar in brown habit, coming at us from an image powerful and contemplative in its immediacy? He beats his breast in penitence while meditating on the book in his hand. The crucifixion and the raw, stormy landscape behind him underline the turbulence in his eyes.

Who can easily withdraw from the hypnotic, direct stare of personages cast before a background which seems to push them forward into our own lived space? The mystery of their faces affects us first, as though to lead us into what remains untold. Such is the *Portrait of a Man with Felt Hat* (circa 1541), where an unpretentious man in simple costume, clasping a large felt hat, strikes a diffident pose with his dishevelled hair and his questioning, unassuming eyes. Such is also the subtle, boldly executed *Portrait of a Gentleman with Gloves* (circa 1543), where the expensive, sober coat, the gold chain, large gold ring, the embroidered white handkerchief and gloves, focus our attention even more onto the tense face with introspective eyes. The intertwining of attire and demeanour makes us ask: "Why is this man so anguished?"

Six months after encountering Lotto's vivid images in Bergamo, I'm stunned in the Grand Palais of Paris by how powerful and delicately wrought they are. On a misty, black

December day, the sensual Italian eyes afford me yet another rebirth. They dispel the spleen I experience in the wet streets. As I move slowly from one painting to the next, I wonder how Lotto escaped censure by the Church for his angels that embody such fleeting wildness and fierce, sensual freedom. Above all though, I wonder why the Roman Catholic Inquisitors did not accuse the portraits of "concupiscence of the eyes," that sin which leads us astray into indiscretion and dispersion? Why are the eyes of these paintings inspecting me so curiously? Why have I been so intent on travelling to Paris for a second viewing of the Lotto exhibit? I think of Nietzsche's phrase "Some travel because they are searching for themselves, others because they want to loose themselves," and am grateful that, after diaspora, art works can gather again at special times in special places. In the French capital Lotto's portraits compel me more strongly than ever not to avert my eyes, but to return their gaze, to pursue more actively the hidden energy that burns in them.

## Lotto's Angels

*Church of San Bernardino, Bergamo*

### I

Not the pensive
wordless pillars of God
with blank eyes and stiff knees

but four naked, haloless
angels bracing the Madonna's throne.
Legs drunk with wind,
arms sweeping eternity down,
shoulders restless rafters —

While outside shuffle sunstruck tourists
forgetting the cool light of Lotto's undressed sky.

## II

He listens, wise eyes scanning
the church's nave.  His slender feet know
winters lived alone, raids on empty roads.
A blue scarf and brown woolen gown
befriend him to peasants.  What is he writing,
crouched below the Virgin's hand?
Does he know what we long for on earth?
Does the flight upsky of those athletic
other messengers arc through his repose?
I murmur, *Show me your writing*,
coax him.  Think *writing* and feed
his pen.  Writing and mystic sweetness.
Maybe now this young angel will sketch
a world where words rise like steam
from dark loam after summer rain.

**Tangible Faith**

*The 1998 Lorenzo Lotto Exposition*

We're transfixed by
    these portraits, light starting
in open faces, after a long night
    beyond the secrecy
of palace and church.

Legends revived
    in the contemplation
of a viewer. How intense
    their gaze,
determined, enigmatic. This biblical

widow, Judith, raising her sword
    and Holofernes'
severed head, before
    a bewildered maid.
How to inhabit that confidence?

The Renaissance world.
    A lady compelling the moon's
course, a gentleman
    clasping his gloves,
a married couple under Eros' yoke.

Eyes prefiguring things to come.
    We're tested by those faces.
And clairvoyance streams from
    Judith's stance, hungry as love,
radiating tangible faith, consenting
    to renewal.

## CARAVAGGIO'S SEVERED HEADS

On a July dawn in 1610 fishermen found a mutilated body on the beach near Port'Ercole in southern Italy. The torrid Mediterranean heat wrapped the dead man in a mantle of light. The day before the man had struggled over the sand to catch a boat for Rome where he might find anonymity, shelter in the crowd. No longer young, covered with scars, anguished and feverish, he hadn't slept for nights as he fled from Naples hunted by hired killers. Before that, he had left Sicily to avoid the vendetta of the Knights of Malta. A whole day on that beach, hounded, he sought a boat, hoping as a drowning man who clings to a plank, then he collapsed: Caravaggio, perhaps the most pivotal artist of his time, had created art at the outer edge; Caravaggio, isolated and destitute, was dead at a bleak outpost. So goes one version of his story.

Even before his violent death, admirers and detractors had obscured his life with multiple legends. Since then, art lovers summon up colourful images when his name is uttered of the violent man, unable to outgrow his addiction to street brawls and criminal activities; the lover of boys, who used prostitutes for models and went to bed with a dagger at his side; the wizard, subject to bottomless fits of rage but able to make shadows speak; the miraculous volcano, who subverted the tradition and anticipated trends to come. These carica-tures all contain a kernel of truth, but they don't alter the fact that the canvases of this genius dazzle us still with their shocking frankness and inimitable power.

Born in 1571 Michelangelo Merisi, he was later called Caravaggio after the village of his birth in the Lombardy of northern Italy. He led a disquieted, homeless life. At nineteen he was already an exile in Rome owing to the death of a drinking companion in Milan. In the Holy City he divided his time between the refined palaces and gardens of aristocratic patrons and the dangerous underworld of streets and brothels. A man with insolent black eyes, he had no respect for rank, lusted for illicit adventures, kept his tongue well-armed for quarrelsome assaults on authority. Arrested and jailed several times, even condemned to death after he supposedly committed murder, Caravaggio was banished from Rome. But not before he had fixed in his mind and art the aggressive and passionate actors of the entire Roman social spectrum: princes, cardinals, derelicts, mercenaries, brawlers and whores. With his departure from the Italian art capital began his restless wandering as a fugitive to Naples, Malta, Sicily; a price on his head, he carefully avoided ambush and hoped for pardon from the Pope. When at last pardon came, it came too late; the truant genius, who had mixed with astonishing brio the profane and the sacred, was dead.

The violence in Caravaggio's character matches stormy 16th century Italy. Never the darling of the popes, who employed armies of artists for their vast building projects, Caravaggio was protected by Cardinal Del Monte and the aristocratic Colonna family. These patrons, specialists of intrigue, private vendettas and wars, were also driven by rebelliousness and appreciated an artist who rethought scriptural iconography. To their eyes, the wildness in Caravaggio's life and art urgently rehearsed the fateful light and dark of the human condition. Nowhere is this more tragically poignant than in the self-portraits Caravaggio introduced, seemingly at random, into his paintings. Moreover, the darkness and anarchic spirit of his canvases reflect the terrors of the era's spiritual and social crises.

The full force of Caravaggio's art is already evident in its trajectory: starting with lyrical, sensuous, delightfully sweet genre paintings of gypsies, musicians and card players, it reaches a dramatic climax in the bold renewals of religious figures. Here Caravaggio's most moving iconographic marvels centre on the theatrical rites of execution, refigure desire, violence and death.

Raised in Luxembourg during World War II, biblical stories were the only heroic literature I knew. From the age of six I heard from nuns and priests, in the then-obligatory religious instruction at school, the sagas of brave men and women from the Old Testament. It never occurred to me when hearing about Judith and Holofernes that some fifty years later I might have a stunning revelation into the inner workings of that drama through a painting. Judith, the beautiful Jewish widow, boldly saves her people from the brutal Assyrian general Holofernes, according to the version I heard. With feminine wile she introduces herself into Holofernes' camp, and while he lies drunk on his bed, she decapitates him, returning triumphantly to the Israelites with her bloody trophy in a sack. She was the perfect symbol of victorious battle against sinners and heretics.

Caravaggio's depiction elicits another dimension: sexual horror. On the canvas no foreground space separates the viewer from the bloody episode; we are not mere spectators, but accomplices to the gory deed. Against the background of the dark red tent, Holofernes is awake as his head is severed, blood jetting from his neck, and Judith, intent in her blow, seems clearly more appalled at her own act than at the naked man she slays. The immediacy of Caravaggio's painting in the dark, enclosed space transforms the scene with the erotic tensions present in all murders. The horror and intimacy of the scene reach a paroxysm in the old servant's stare as she waits to bag the head, in the arched, naked body of Holofernes as he clutches the sheet in agony, and above all in the frozen frown on Judith's face as she determinedly hacks at Holofernes' neck, the sword in her right hand, his hair in her left hand. In this killing, moans of lust mingle with cries of death. Violence tenses the hand movements and the facial expressions of the three actors. Caravaggio's image is not merely a representation of the triumphant and chaste widow Judith who pre-figures the Virgin Mary, it is a drama of desire and death.

Caravaggio repeatedly returned to decapitation in many of his paintings. Did that interest stem merely from the ferocious measures against outlaws in the Rome of his day: capital punishment decreed for criminals as young as fourteen; the heads of thousands of marauders exposed at Sant Angelo bridge, and the Pope lamenting that in 1587 only seven thousand bandits were executed by beheading? Or did those violent paintings echo the mysterious nothingness which undergirds human existence?

The tragic splendour of Judith and Holofernes is no less glowing in *Salomè with the Head of John the Baptist*, an image painted in 1609, the year before the artist's death. Here Caravaggio transmutes the biblical tale of the seductive dancing girl who asks King Herod for the head of the saintly

man into an austere meditation on human grief. Three figures
rise out of a pool of black, no action mars the still, contem-
plative mood. Salomè stands on the left in a red mantle
holding the brass basin with the severed head. Her eyes, full
of melancholy, look away. It's the ancient servant woman
whose eyes are lowered to the dish with John's head. She is
almost joined to the top of Salomè's body — as stony witness,
or other side of Salomè's soul. Bared shoulders turned away,
the executioner, a handsome young man, glances sadly back
at his victim. How powerfully the four heads are trapped in
their own darkness: three captured in the infinite sorrow of
life, one in death.

 *David with the Head of Goliath* (1606) continues
Caravaggio's re-interpretations of the Old Testament. The
Bible tells us that after having killed the giant Goliath with a
stone from his sling, David cut off his head. Against stark
darkness, Caravaggio depicts the boy standing half length,
sword glinting in one hand, and in the other the severed head
of his antagonist. Goliath's forehead is wounded, his neck
bloody, one eye stares with anguish into the void, while the
open mouth is frozen with its last gasp for breath. The
severed head is projected far forward toward the viewer.
Both figures rise from the closed dark of a terrible event, the
boy looking down with tender regret onto the murdered man.
Given that his name means "beloved," it's appropriate David
does not appear a vicious henchman. More startling, the head
he holds bears the ravaged features of Caravaggio himself,
who through this self-portrait imagines his own execution.
The boy-assassin, with the slender classical body and the
subtly sorrowful face embodying the light of life, looks down
onto Goliath / Caravaggio, who through death, ensnares us in

his tragedy.

This depiction harkens back to the astounding severed head of the *Medusa* which Caravaggio painted onto a poplar shield in 1598. There he worked with the myth of the snake-haired monster who petrified humans with her hideous yet bewitching gaze; the Medusa was beheaded by Perseus, who avoided her direct gaze by viewing her through a mirror. Caravaggio's image, again a self-portrait, shows the Medusa crying with terror as she contemplates her end, the blood falling already hardened from her cut neck. The depiction's haunting power resides again in the way the Medusa's head, without anger or scorn, juts toward the viewers, as if still to enthral and stun them with her rolling eyeballs. Does the petrifying force of the gaze turned onto the Gorgon herself extend to those who look inward to wallow in introspection?

Fifty-five years after my first religious instruction in Luxembourg, I meet Caravaggio's reworkings of the Christian figures in Bergamo's Accademia Carrara. On a hot July day, the sun throwing daggers of light into the courtyard and street where Italians and other tourists are patiently crawling along in a line-up two hours long, we enter the inner sanctum via a side door, and are immediately stunned by paintings hung in otherwise pitch black rooms; well-placed spot lights underscored their moral complexities, their questions and revelations. I find in them an injunction to take "the less travelled road" with them and their creator.

The Medusa's terror hits me hard; it readies me to look closer at *Ursula Transfixed* (1610), in which Caravaggio achieved another moving re-interpretation of an early Christian legend. After slaughtering eleven thousand Christian virgins, the companions of the beautiful princess

Ursula, the Hun chief falls in love with her and proposes marriage. When she refuses, Ursula is killed. Rather than concentrating, as predecessors had done, on the mass-murder of the virgins, Caravaggio distils the essence of the story into its final episode. He catches the main actors, three quarter size, at the moment of paroxysm. Clad in a ruby red cloak, Ursula clasps her wound as she bends a white mask-like face down over her breast, into which the mad Hun has just shot his deadly arrow at point blank range. She appears composed, yet puzzled. Above her, in self-portrait, Caravaggio's face, aghast, measures the desolation of the bleak event. Most surprising, though, is the representation of the murderous leader of the Huns. Magnificently decked out in a crimson attire and ornate breastplate, he appears as anything but a monstrous barbarian. A smallish older man, who had been mocked by the eleven thousand virgins and rejected by Saint Ursula, he appears infinitely sad as he contemplates the full horror of his crime and the consummation of Ursula's martyrdom. The spectator too is subjected to the dread of death and the pathos of revenge.

As we move slowly through the dark rooms, from painting to painting, we cross stretches of new land. In the silent gathering, we feel focused and transformed by the images; they afford a glance into the brutal realities of human actions. Long after we leave the exhibition for a sumptuous meal, we remain so profoundly stirred that tokens of Caravaggio's images weave through our conversation. The creative triumphs and personal catastrophe of this visionary artist so expands our hearts that, even when we are a continent away, his painterly performances sharpen the chiaroscuro of our lives; charting a path through the shadows which menace every day everywhere, Caravaggio's paintings take on an increasingly consoling power.

## Untethered in Paradise

Italy:  an all-consuming work of art
that fires the nailed-down Northern mind.
We become untethered;
dawn takes off, night
says *buona notte*.  An open jewelry box,
filled with glittering words, gems ablaze.

We swoop through crowds lost in paradise —
laughter outflung, greetings and pleas.
All afternoon we retrace Caravaggio's life,
competing with cardinals and whores,
so intently we're already dropping off
heaven's rim, onto beaches where fishermen
at day break pick up the dead.

**The Naked Heart**

*Caravaggio Exhibit, 2000*

At noon Bergamo craves darkness,
the lit-up faces of women
remove me from chatter, cancel
thought.   In the Carrara Gallery

crowds jostle me close to eyes that
sweep away holy guile, bloody deeds,
their gaze not an upward swoon,
but reinventions of the naked heart.

Heretic, I too inhabit fierce secrets,
this side of God's hand.   Caravaggio's
Judith, Ursula, Salome open
a hunger tempered by composure, bent

heads — intersections I long to traverse,
centuries of glances, gestures clarified,
ready to play.

**Caravaggio's Medusa**  (circa 1598)

Her glance rummaging in death for something —
no one can guess — an answer
forgotten for this reversal.

A woman swayed in doubt, staring
through our poses, masks.
Those reprieves from anguish and future.

Her eyes lucent
looming over a pain loud
as life, obscure, abloom.

# V

## HOLLAND:

## THE PAINTER OF READERS & WRITERS

## VERMEER'S THEATRE OF CALLIGRAPHY

What a shock to be told that all tickets were sold for the Vermeer exhibition that summer in The Hague. In January 1996 this was. The industry of cultural tourism in Europe had already gained such momentum that convoys of buses were descending upon every possible pilgrimage site. Planning agents bought up tickets months in advance, and then herded hungry hoards to the grazing grounds. In a letter that same January, an American friend recounted her experience of the Vermeer exhibit at the National Gallery in Washington, D.C. She had waited an hour and a half in the snow to gain admittance. Once inside, the paintings had gripped her so strongly that she retrospectively offered up in sacrifice her frozen limbs to the splendour of the Dutch master's art. For about a week after receiving that letter, I felt myself marooned in the wrong hinterland. Then I ordered from the Gallery in Washington the catalogue of the exhibition and intoxicated myself with reproductions.

Five of the twenty-three exhibited paintings I had previously seen in their regular homes, the Rijksmuseum of Amsterdam, the Mauritshuis of The Hague, and the Louvre in Paris. On those occasions, I recognized in Vermeer's *The Little Street* (1657-1658) an elemental scene, half-dreamed, half-real, of lost paradise. How often had I crossed the cobblestones of that quiet little street of Delft to the wooden doorways of the red brick houses! Sometimes I greeted the maid servant in the adjacent passageway and also the seated woman, absorbed in her hand-work. Intermittently I had even been one of the two children bent over at the sidewalk's edge, engrossed in a game. Life in small northern European towns was characterized, until the middle of the last century, by industry in and around the home. Vermeer's painting brings back, below slightly clouded skies, streets without traffic, with the ambience of an outdoor dwelling and living space. Looking at that image, I wonder whether art endows formerly quotidian lives with a poetic eternity or whether time casts a beautiful permanence over scenes one remembers or dreams.

Proust called Vermeer's *View of Delft* (1660-1661) "the most beautiful painting in the world." In that city-on-canvas one can indeed imagine the household scenes of his other paintings. The humble rooms with pitted bare walls in which *The Milkmaid* (1658-1660) pours with steadfast gaze and measured movements. She is not an insignificant maid, but a heroine of striking physical and moral dignity. Her massive form, her strong arms provide life-sustaining milk and bread. Simple warmth and devotion make up her authority.

*The Lacemaker* (1669-1670), creator of finery, also practised her craft in one of Delft's streets. A picture of clear vision, of total industrious attention, she bends over intently, holding tautly the bobbins and pins, while next to her rests her prayer book or small Bible. *The Girl with a Pearl Earring* (1665-1666) inhabited yet another house of Delft. Her unique face subsequently earned her the name the "Dutch Mona Lisa." She rises timelessly out of an undefined darkness. Her parted mouth, her pure eyes, soft skin and fluid tear-drop pearl earring captivate us. Like the quiet little street and all the still rooms of Vermeer's images, this woman gives her viewers silence as a gift.

But opulent, 17th century Delft is not merely filled up with houses of rich, patrician merchants, dwellings ruled by domesticity, thrift and conservative manners. Vermeer's transparent and discrete depictions of interior spaces adumbrate secrets below the luminous surfaces. Why does this exact, hyper-realist painter call out to us to read his images? Is it his devotion to objects? The moral tenor in his people? The domestic intimacy of his scenes? Or is it that he caught things and people before they disappeared?

For me the quiet moments of meditation which Vermeer's numerous scenes of writing and reading letters portray are part of his theatre of calligraphy. Who has not been moved by *Woman in Blue Reading a Letter* (1663-1664)? An overpowering visual impact, an extraordinarily reflective mood emanates from this self-contained woman. She stands simply in the quiet privacy of her room, engrossed in her letter, in front of a map suspended on the wall. Did her letter come from a place marked on that map? Is she expecting someone or something from far away?

Or is she the sister of *The Geographer* (1668-1669), the map maker surprised by Vermeer in his professional stance? In one hand he holds the divider, the instrument used to mark distances between land masses, with the other hand he leans on a book. Maps, charts and a globe, the achievements of his profession, sit around him as silent yet prominent witnesses. His face, turned to the window, has a searching expression. His mathematical and navigational skills will lead beyond mere dreams of discovering passages through new lands, across unknown coastlines. Ultimately they'll take him outside of his study, to chart a course through the future.

Often in Vermeer paintings women epitomize the spirit of

dislocation—perhaps of longing and of travel—through their writing and reading of letters. In 1665, ten years before his death, the artist painted the magnificent image *A Lady Writing*. In her penumbral room, this woman, in yellow fur-trimmed jacket, is seated at a desk. She pauses in her writing and looks up with a smile. By whom has her calm activity been interrupted? By us, the viewers? Or is she awaiting a visitor in her tranquil private chamber? No answer will distract from the lovely reflectiveness of this scene. No letter written by Vermeer himself informs us. His paintings point to the mystery of this ritual. If there is a story to be told, it is told by implication only.

We need not fabricate stories around *The Love Letter* (1669-1670) either. Here we look through the doorway of a darkened anteroom into an elegant private space, where a mistress stops playing her cittern to look questioningly at her maid who holds a letter in her right hand. Our glance traverses a blue and white tiled floor beyond shoes and a broom cast down at the entry. The psychological impact of the scene strikes first. The mistress' eyes seem worried. Are her concerns unfounded? After all, the maid smiles in kindly anticipation. Has the letter brought on an anxiety? Has there been neglect of domestic responsibilities? Vermeer's non-narrative art does not reveal the secrets of his world. We can only suspect some hidden domain beyond the reality depicted, the pure light that alters the figures and objects of his interiors.

Vermeer's last known masterpiece of his theatre of calligraphy is *Lady Writing a Letter with her Maid* (1670). This glorious achievement, painted five years prior to the painter's death, shows two women in an austere and elegant interior — the mistress writing, the maid by the window looking out dreamily. This subdued scene in muted colours, with its self-contained shapes and people, highlights the contrast between the two women's activities. The statuesque maid, in her folded, floor-length, brownish-grey dress is reminiscent of a nun. The mistress, in her bright white and yellow garb, leans forward energetically as though pulled into an adventure. The dynamic spatial configurations draw the viewer's eye from maid to mistress, to the crumpled letter on the black and white marble floor and back again to the maid. Is the mistress writing in response to that letter? Through the stances of the two women Vermeer's genius focuses on a longing to be elsewhere within the present surroundings. The activities of these two women embody the spirit of writing. Longing and writing save them in their here and now. They are not idealized Madonnas hankering after a salvation elsewhere. Writing, reading and longing, the concentrated gestures of eyes, hand and imagination are performed in the quiet rooms of the house — the light received there from the outside is reflected by that produced inside.

I think of Vermeer as a painter of readers and writers, an artist of journeys and destinations. Words blow to and from far-away countries, arrow in and out of well-kept rooms bathed alternately in the sunlight or penumbra of the everyday. The launching and landing place of these peregrinating words is the home. There, women take charge of and are claimed by the household. The letters they read and write are acts of domestic care. All roads in Vermeer's paintings lead to the home's adventures of undiscovered or lost miracles. His women, as they pour over letters, are also voyaging into the unknown. They make me feel that a world without the light of writing is impossible.

**Household Tools**

*The 1996 Johannes Vermeer Exposition*

We walk into these
    paintings, an intimate
little street, through passageways
    the inner courtyards
of quotidian concerns.

Stories sealed
    by the hourglass
of silence.  How intense
    their lives are,
resonant, serene.  This figure,

Vermeer's milkmaid, raising
    her red arms
over dark bread,
    to pour milk.
Let's prolong that light.

The century of discovery.
    A woman gazing into her
mirror, a writer
    transfixing her viewer,
a geographer searching the outside.

Faces bundled with desire.
Can we grow those eyes?
And the milk keeps flowing from
strong hands, stained as sunsets,
handling household tools, making
everything possible.

# VI

## CANADA / LUXEMBOURG:

## FELLOW WORKERS

## COLVILLE'S INSIDES / OUTSIDES

Two recent paintings by Alex Colville summon up two scenes elemental in his work. *Living Room* (1999-2000) takes the viewer inside his domestic principality, while *Surveyor* (2001) opens out onto the pristine kingdom of his Maritime outdoors. The first is remarkable for its subdued directness and profound simplicity: the woman playing the piano, the man listening as he looks at us, the dog sleeping, an understated yet strikingly warm light. The second for its marshy dyke lands, steeped in brown mud and fresh greens, a view which the brightly clad young woman surveyor will carry in her memory once her measuring is completed. We can call forth these scenes and be reminded that with them we have entered two vast landscapes of the imagination.

"I only do small things," Colville told me when he showed me the atelier in his new house a few years ago. In *Living Room* (40 x 56.5 cm) and *Surveyor* (36 x 63.2 cm) that statement has ripened parabolically. His paintings look deceptively small and modest, yet they are emphatically monumental. They remain unpretentious like those of the classical masters, with whom he shares an admirable technical skill, a firm sense of balance, a love of detail and a complex visual clarity.

*Living Room* and *Surveyor* have the resonance and texture of Colville's other work: simultaneously modern and classical with a startling intellectual clarity. The result of a lifetime of thinking about art and how human experience embraces it, these two paintings demonstrate Colville's approach to reality — his curiosity, precision and affection as he seeks the elusive. He subtly confronts our immediate Canadian reality by juxtaposing it with a universal experience, a feat he achieves through his cool, economical style devoid of grand effects or artificial explosions. The surfaces of his images are so cleanly and naturally rendered that one might miss their meditative and emblematic dimension. The spaces in all of Colville's paintings arise and are brought home to us in such a way that their insides and outsides speak intently.

However, the spaces are performed both with a deceptive immediacy and with a sly illumination: this is the benchmark of Colville's style. For instance in *Living Room* the meditative quality of playing and listening to piano music comes through the quasi-religious tension between the woman's demeanor and the dour pose of the man. In *Surveyor* the tension between the youthful girl dressed in shorts, construction helmet, and fluorescent vest, and a trade as old as the Egyptians guides us toward enigmatic conjunctions.

Colville's masterpieces always plumb the discreet ambiguity, ironic playfulness and quiet eroticism of their subject. His *Living Room*, ostensibly a peaceful domestic scene, might suggest that man, woman and dog are individually facing, in a gathered way, not just one particular evening but the ultimate one. A parallel subtlety is at work in *Surveyor*. This seemingly representational work creates its special effect by placing a young woman into the foreground against a vast Maritime seashore where the tides erase the boundaries established by humans. We could understand the painting as an allegory of calculative achievement, while in reality it praises a young woman's vocational rootedness in the earth. Colville's art suggests, in its ambiguity, radically different meanings simultaneously.

Why do these two paintings move us so powerfully? Are they an asylum of sanity and beauty within the frenzied consumerism and pop culture of our time? Exemplary in Colville's paintings is a love for reality, life and order. Could they represent a moral code and an image of civilization? Do they spring from an unshakable faith in the things of this world, a conviction that things are substantive even though they exist only in constant disintegration and, finally, annihilation? Do these paintings attempt to fix the world in its substance before it evaporates? Does Colville's art confirm the existence of our world with the intent of fulfilling its miracle?

Constant in Colville's art is a special appetite for his native Canadian landscape and for scenes of everyday life. Since painting is a craft for him, he must believe in the purposefulness of his works. Thus the inspired seriousness with which he affirms his immediate visible reality. In our epoch of speed and dispersion this fidelity to the concrete opens our eyes, leading us to the things-in-themselves. Yet Colville, as a creator, is also a supremely reflective painter. His work addresses the problem of realistic evocation. Rather than describing the world, *Living Room* and *Surveyor* address it affectionately and intimately. Faithful to what is seen, the paintings speak the language of reality itself. We viewers are stopped by the meticulous glittering northern light, the enormous Canadian skies, the brown sea, but we also look hard at the calm stillness of a living room where a woman makes music and a man listens. And finally we are inspired to cross the hidden barrier of everyday experience, entering into things radiating discretely and luminously in an endless conversation of insides and outsides, interiors and exteriors.

I go to Colville for an absolutely contemporary yet very ancient light. His reverent, unsentimental vision keeps open the mystery within our daily rituals and loves. The Canadian experience flows steadily out of his paintings, like the great tidal rivers. His art leads me to think seriously about my own life and to give thanks when it works.

**Radiant Hush**

*Alex Colville's Living Room, 1999-2000*

When you stepped into the living room
past the seated, stern-faced man
onto the caramel rug,
past the dog curled in sleep,
you stood near the piano, still,
listening for muted arpeggios
and did not address the woman playing.

Now you keep your appointment with that night,
its radiant hush within the music's sounds, open
its unknown lights and the shadows serenely waiting
    outside.
Closely attentive to these dwellers,
your eyes touch their quiet faces.

**Surveyor**

*after Alex Colville's 2001 painting*

In the painting, I'm the young surveyor —
do not hear the foghorn
float barges of sadness
over land, a body blind,
deaf for this world,
but wear a yellow helmet, shorts,
peer into the transit's precise eye,
my tripod and fluorescent
vest plant me
into Fundy's tidal beds,
a Nile's overflow;
I map — chocolate shoulders and thighs,
damns and curves —
the ocean's property, the dikes' memory.
I fix the currents' ancient faces
after the flood,
forget washed-out hopes;
in the painting
I leave prints free as the flow.

PAINTING: NOT A PROFESSION, BUT A RELIGION

Paintings are underway toward someone. Sometimes they find us in a museum. Other times at home, when we are fully alert, studying the catalogue of an exhibition, a reproduction can act as a message in the bottle sent out by the original work. For a moment the secret of the painting addresses us; we become its heartland.

In May 1999, on a Sunday afternoon, I traversed the park of Luxembourg's Villa Vauban, an old patrician dwelling turned into a gallery for classical and contemporary art. I was on my way to view the exhibition *Light, Shadow and Passion: Ten Years of Painting in Mallorca.* Until then, the Luxembourg artist, Gust Graas, had been unknown to me. But that day a lively young woman guided the few visitors through the rooms, stopping every so often in front of one of the large abstract canvases, not to explicate it didactically, but to bring it into focus by reading extracts from the painter's book *Notes from the Atelier.* That text consisted of reflections about art: "Painting is not a profession but a religion." "Blue is space... Kandinsky compared light blue to the timbre of a flute, dark blue to the sonority of an organ." Or thoughts about daily wrestles with the Muse: "I like my last painting: a vision of one instant of unburdened happiness, result of a passing constellation that came and went out of nothingness." Or musings about fulfilment: "After a series of dark paintings, I feel like moving, leaving, celebrating freely and painting the sunny side of life, to make joy visible."

Even though the paintings themselves overwhelmed me immediately, the intense, generous and sure-footed voice of the artist's writing grabbed my imagination. I attempted to procure a copy of *Notes from the Atelier* at local book stores, but to no avail. After some detective work, I found the artist's address, sent him a poem I had written about his exposition and asked to buy a copy of his book. Four days later the book arrived in the mail, with a small painting entitled *Bonjour la poésie*. On its back was written: "Dear Poetess, thanks for having communed with my canvases. They must have swelled with joy. That's encouraging." I answered with a second poem. And thus began a correspondence with an artist whom I was not to meet for some time. He would send me small paintings, woodcuts or drawings from Mallorca, one of his sites of work, or from Luxembourg, his homeland; I would respond with poems from my quiet outpost near Fundy Bay. Whenever his sun-drenched images from Europe arrived in the snowy north, the ice thawed as if struck by a warm southern breeze, and the well of words flowed.

Long after I had received Gust Graas' letter-paintings, even after my poem-responses were flying to the old continent, the images kept me in their grasp, taking me back to the large abstract canvases hung in the Villa Vauban. That spring Sunday in Luxembourg, I had longed for something ecstatic. The non-figurative images sustained me in my longing. They pressed me to leave the world within and open to the world outside in new ways. They spoke to the pilgrim in me, who sets forth playfully to be renewed. It was as though I had paused in open air, as in Mallarmé's poem "Sea

Breeze":

> To be amidst unknown foam and skies! . . .
> Raise anchor for exotic lands! . . .
> But, o my heart, listen to the sailors' song!

The thematic texture of Graas' canvases also triggered the return of Mallarmé's sonnet "To the mere concern of journeying," the invocation to venture beyond time and space to a distant horizon, intoxicated by the waves' foam, leaving behind constrictions to dart with excitement into unknown vistas. Not knowing the painter, having only seen him kneeling intently over his paintings in the catalogue's photograph, I transferred the focus from the paintings' energy to the quiet Vasco da Gamma of Mallarmé's poem. Yes, Graas' smile was reminiscent of Vasco's steady and luminous face. Here was an explorer who held his direction and did not deviate from his purpose. Unbeknownst to me at the time, I had already embarked on an adventure in abstract art.

What was in store for me? Colours were the first primitive pleasures that made things happen. They came alive in my eyes creating an incantatory rhythm, enacting what they pictured. This painter was above all a shaper of colours; his world spoke in them:

> Colour is the surest path from the senses to the feelings
> and back to depiction. Colour is matter. Vivified by the
> painter, it becomes a magic powder which fills invisible
> vials with its substance, enlivens unknown form, makes
> space perceivable, endows structure to powers, catches
> time, makes one sing with joy and die in a death struggle.

Indeed, the colours enlarged my eyes, guided them into the dynamic emergence of creation from chaos. Rimbaud's poem

"Vowels" seemed recreated here:

> A black, E white, I red, U green, O blue, vowels,
> One day I'll say your latent births.

Colours conjoined in the universal language that poets had
dreamed about. In their innocence they brought out a world
in elemental becoming.

The colours invited me to lyrical improvisations. At
times bold reds, oranges and blacks glowed like crystals. At
other times shimmering tides of blue and green grabbed me
into their dance through vast spaces. Then, too, softly-tuned
blues and greys carried me into their reverie. For a moment
houses, skies, lighthouses, the domes of sacred habitations
could be divined, adumbrations of a spiritual climate. These
colours primed me to follow Rimbaud: "Welcome all the
influx of vigour and real tenderness. And, at dawn, armed
with ardent patience, you will enter splendid cities." Since
Graas hardly ever gives titles to his paintings, the viewer is
free to recompose the works with aroused desire.

For my second visit to Graas' exposition, I carried
Feuerbach's dictum: "To understand a painting you need a
chair." These words quieted my legs which tired during the
several hours of intense looking. The polyphonic canvases
alerted my senses to move from the visible to the invisible
and back again. Animated by these visions, I breathed
deeper, remembering what I had read in *Notes from the
Atelier*: "Whether consciously or unconsciously, the painter
has always assumed the task of visionary. He compliments
the work of the philosopher, the poet and the musician." The
canvases awakened me to new possibilities. I was liberated
from temporal and spatial safety into an unknown. Was this

fulfilment? The bedrock of being? Or anticipation?

And what of my poem-painting correspondence with Gust Graas? Was it a nostalgic return to a time of pen pals? Far from it. The images he sends are much more than fugitive guests or background noise in our house. They embody for my husband and me Graas' intent "to make happiness felt in all its dimensions." They inhabit our eyes and conversations for days, tokens from a fellow-worker who also wrote: "Painting means uncovering, giving a new direction to life." Now framed on our walls, some are messages in the bottle, vehicles for cooperating in a playful quest.

## New Year's Wishes 2001

*from Pollença*

Phantasmagoria:  A
phalanx of blue
blooms.

(sea and sky
are flower bells,
just as indigo).

Each pair the eyes of a god.
The whole a throng, a kingdom
to discover, invade:

above
all crystals, violets,
forget-me-nots.

**Painter at Home**

*Reading Notes d'Atelier*

Rushing through the atelier to open
shutters, doors, dispell
humid air, to meet
the canvas begun yesterday.  He
touches the painting, a dark fruit
made hand-hold, rubs
its velvet heart.  The place
for bending thought
in pilgrimage to un-named things.  Now
the testing anguish —
that everything is born to die,
blow and fold into ash.
A frail vision dreaming, and the work
unfinished.

Braided colours, lines awakening.
Furtive bliss.

***In Murnau I hope to encounter Kandinsky*** — Gust Graas

Everywhere doors and
we are knocking.

Gabriele, whom
he abandoned,
we cannot find.

Two artists and two
journeys,
we recreate.

"They're gone," say the houses.

After his departure, the mirage
of departure —

a trace never erased from Gabriele's paintings,
as Bach is sometimes
played in old cathedrals:
We drink stained-
glass light and, the fugues
over, tune our ears
to a lavender silence; the fury
receded, a bold
sunset in minds
still seized by the heat.

## Works Cited or Consulted

Baudelaire, Charles. *Oeuvres complètes*. Paris: Édition de la Pléiade, 1961.

Butler, Ruth. *Rodin: The Shape of Genius*. New Haven: Yale University Press, 1993.

Callow, Philip. *Lost Earth: A Life of Cézanne*. Chicago: Ivan R. Dee, 1995.

Rosenberg, Pierre & Temperini, Renaud. *Chardin*. Munich, London, New York: Prestel, 2000.

*Alberto Giacometti*. New York: Abrams, 2001.

*Giovanni Giacometti*. Winterthur: Kunstmuseum, 1996.

Graas, Gust. *Notes d'Atelier et Peintures*. Luxembourg: Imprimerie St. Paul, 1993.

Heidegger, Martin. *Gesammtausgabe, Band 13*. Frankfurt: Vittorio Klostermann, 1983.

Langdon, Helen. *Caravaggio: A Life*. New York: Farrar, Straus & Giroux, 1998.

*Lorenzo Lotto: Rediscovered Master of the Renaissance*. New Haven & London: Yale University Press, 1997.

Mallarmé, Stéphane. *Oeuvres complètes*. Paris: Édition de la Pléiade, 1963.

*Monet in the 20th Century*. New Haven: Yale University Press, 1998.

Nietzsche, Friedrich. *Die Unschuld des Werdens*. Stuttgart: Alfred Kröner, 1978.

Rimbaud, Arthur. *Oeuvres complètes*. Paris: Édition de la Pléiade, 1963.

*Johannes Vermeer*. New Haven & London: Yale University Press, 1995.

Whitman, Walt. *Leaves of Grass*. New York: Norton, 1965.

## Critics:

Travelling across Welch's work and going back to it again and again is perhaps best described by the fashionable metaphor of the web. This is not the web of electronic communication, but the web of culture and books. Progressively, we are drawn into it and invited to share her dialogue with a host of characters and situations. Gradually a world, at once new and familiar, emerges from a sea of images, sounds and rhythms.

— Marie-Anne Hansen-Pauly

Welch shifts smoothly from Europe to New Brunswick, angels to tourists, nuns to eroticism . . . giving us an ever-growing, increasingly coherent tapestry of experience from a rich, humane, and fascinating life, from a mind sceptical about contemporary society but devout within the worlds of nature, art and friends.

— Richard Lemm

Welch's concise lingering word combinations burn bright, clear images on our mental retinas and stun us again and again on every page . . . induce deep, prolonged pleasure.          — Mylène Rizzi

Each one of Welch's poems is a journey into experience, an expression of love, a spiritual renewal, a perpetual gift.

— Michael O. Nowlan

Welch's poetry reflects her quest for spiritual enlightenment and her awareness of nature as a source of inner peace and fulfillment . . . Many of her poems are inspired by her deep connection with the arts and literature, but Welch also observes the everyday existence of ordinary people with compassion and understanding, with a wisdom that comes from inner strength and makes room for a consoling faith in humanity.          — Anna Foschi Ciampolini

115

**About the Author**

Liliane Welch is the author of seventeen collections of poems, most recently *Unlearning Ice* (2001). She has co-authored two volumes of literary criticism on modern French poetry, *Emergence: Baudelaire, Mallarmé, Rimbaud;* and *Address: Rimbaud, Mallarmé, Butor.* She has published a book of essays and memoirs, *Seismographs,* and a work of travel prose, *Frescoes.* Her writings have been widely anthologized and translated into French, German and Italian. Her many honours include the Bressani and Alfred Bailey Prizes. She belongs to the Institut Grand Ducal of Luxembourg, her country of birth. Liliane Welch teaches at Mount Allison University in Sackville, New Brunswick, Canada.

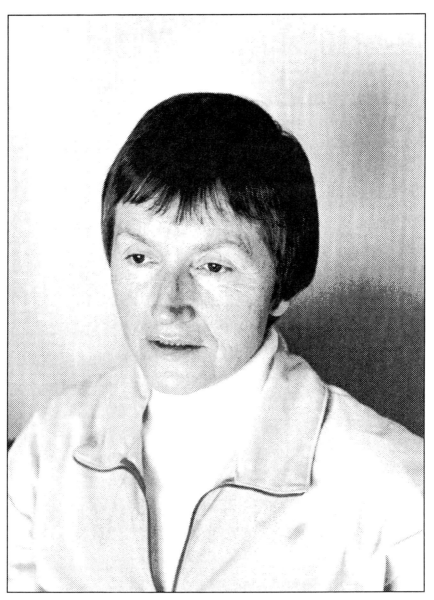

Liliane Welch

MEMBER OF SCABRINI MEDIA

Quebec, Canada
2002